Althusser's Marxism

Pluto **Press**

Alex Callinicos

Althusser's Marxism

Second impression May 1976

First published 1976 by Pluto Press Limited
Unit 10 Spencer Court, 7 Chalcot Road, London NW1 8LH
Copyright © Pluto Press 1976
ISBN 0 904383 02 4
Printed by The Camelot Press Limited, Southampton
Designed by Richard Hollis, GrR

Contents

Preface

Many people need to be thanked for their part in this essay: Eric Cameron, Allin Cottrell, Tony Dodd, Chris Harman, Alan Montefiore, Mike Rosen and Bruce Young, without whom I would understand Althusser even less than I do; Mike Kidron for suggesting I write this essay and Richard Kuper for patiently nursing it; Colin Barker, Jim Grealey and Mike McKenna for their comments on drafts. All would disclaim responsibility for the result, for which I am solely to blame. It is dedicated to the late Imre Lakatos.

Alex Callinicos
December 1975

Introduction

Louis Althusser's claim to our attention is as a Marxist and it is as a Marxist that he must be judged. What he writes of *For Marx* is true of all his work:

> These texts must be taken for what they are. They are *philosophical* essays, the first stages of a long-term investigation, preliminary results which obviously demand correction; this investigation concerns the specific nature of the principles of the science and philosophy founded by Marx. However, these philosophical essays do not derive from a merely erudite or speculative investigation. They are, *simultaneously*, interventions in a definite conjuncture.[1]

The character of this political conjuncture is clearly stated in the same text, and in various other passages in Althusser's work. It is essentially the crisis of post-war Stalinism, the crisis brought about in the world communist movement by the attempt, beginning in 1956 with the Twentieth Congress of the Communist Party of the Soviet Union, to redefine the character of the movement.[2] We shall discuss this crisis, and its relation to the philosophical problems Althusser has dealt with, below.[3]

My intention to take Althusser on his own terms, that is, as a Marxist, settles my approach in this essay. Most importantly, it settles what this essay is not. It is not a study of Althusser's work as part of the intellectual trends popularly heaped together under the title of structuralism (despite the disclaimers of many of structuralism's alleged chief proponents, including Althusser himself). Nor is it a study of Althusser's philosophy in relation to the development of modern French or even European philosophy.[4] It is an attempt to place Althusser in his context within the Marxist tradition and to determine his contribution to that tradition.

This approach has a set of problems all its own. For, what is the

Marxist tradition? To identify it with a selection of texts, as a body of doctrine, opens the way to the worst sort of dogmatism. In any case, this identification would presuppose the existence of principles governing the selection and these principles would be by no means self-evident. Thus, do we include Stalin or Trotsky as part of the Marxist tradition, or neither, or both? This is not merely an academic question, but has a very clear-cut political implication. Yet if the choice is not to be an arbitrary one, dictated by the political needs of the moment, we require some objective standpoint from which to make judgements.

On the other hand, to identify the Marxist tradition with the Marxist method, as Lukacs does,[5] is to open us to the danger of pre-judging the issues that Althusser deals with. For, if we were to go beyond *defining* Marxism in terms of its method to characterising this method, we would be entering the whole area of the Althusser debate, which centres precisely around the problem of method.

This is a problem inherent in our subject. Indeed, we shall return to it when we discuss the circle upon which Althusser's system rests.[6] We can only cope with it now by stipulating the terms in which we are going to approach Althusser. I will not argue for my solution, which is neither original nor anything more than provisional. It is to characterise Marxism as *the theory and practice of proletarian revolution*. The peculiarity of Marxism as a scientific theory lies in the fact that it serves as the instrument of the working-class in its struggle to free itself from capitalist exploitation and oppression, the instrument that, in the hands of a party that grows out of and relates to the self-activity of the proletariat, can serve as the guide on the road to revolution.

There are defects in this formulation. It is too vague for one thing. This need not be a serious fault: we can sharpen it by reference to historical examples and analogies where necessary. More seriously, it is completely dogmatic. I have made no attempt to justify it. This, however, is a fault which I hope will disappear in the course of this essay, since, as we shall see, one important feature of Althusser's work is the light it throws on the relation between Marxist theory and the class struggle.[7]

I shall now outline the course of my argument. I shall first

8

attempt to develop the political importance of the questions raised by Marxist philosophy. I shall then go on to look at Althusser's philosophy as an answer to these questions, first expounding it systematically then examining it critically. The analysis will then be extended beyond the theory as such to the political positions it reflects. Finally, I shall try to draw the strands together by judging Althusser's work in the light of its contribution to the Marxist tradition, that is, to Marxism as the theory and practice of proletarian revolution.

A final word before proceeding. As Althusser himself would say, no reading is innocent; plainly put, every interpretation involves its own theoretical and political presuppositions. I must plead guilty in this respect. My attitude towards Althusser combines sufficient respect for his work to want to make sense of it as a whole and over time, and sufficient reservations, particularly at the political level, to wish to disentangle the errors it contains. In writing this essay, as ought to be clear, I have sometimes shared Althusser's prejudices and assumptions. This is particularly so as far as what I have called Hegelian Marxism is concerned. There is no shame in this; my treatment of Hegelian Marxism is far less summary and polemical than what Althusser has suffered at the hands of Marxist and non-Marxist opponents alike.

At the same time, this essay is not an apologia for Althusser. While he has made significant contributions to an understanding of Marxism which I shall detail, his overall position is not one that can be held by a consistent revolutionary. I have been puzzled by a persistent objection to the effect that there is a contradiction between accepting elements of a theory and refusing to subscribe to it as a whole. Logically this is certainly not the case. From a philosophical point of view, providing the relation between the incorrect and correct elements that enables them to co-exist within one theory is spelled out, we can forget about this 'contradiction'. I have not hesitated to belabour Althusser where he is slipshod, inconsistent or just plain wrong. The problem with Althusser's reception, in Britain at least, has been partly a dogmatic and uncritical acceptance or rejection of his work and partly the eclectic juxtaposition of great undigested lumps of Althusser with similar doses of Lukacs or Sartre. I have tried to avoid these traps.

9

1. Marxism and Philosophy

Engels and the Marxism of the Second International

The peculiar situation of Marxist philosophy is well known. After the works of the early and mid 1840s, culminating in *The German Ideology*, where Marx and Engels settled 'accounts with . . . (their) former philosophical conscience'[1], Marx deals explicitly with philosophical questions only in asides or in straightforward polemic.[2] When the political situation in the German socialist movement made it necessary to develop an overall Marxist philosophical position, the task fell upon Engels in *Anti-Dühring*. It is therefore with Engels that any discussion of the problems of Marxist philosophy must begin.

Marx and Engels had from the 1840s onwards clearly underlined what they saw as demarcating their theory from any other socialist theory: its scientific character. Previously, socialists had put forward a moral critique of the unjust and oppressive condition of the working class under capitalism and had juxtaposed to this an ideal form of society – the ideal to be realised either by some sort of gradual metabolic process of co-operation or persuasion, or by the violent action of the few. Breaking with this tradition, Marx and Engels developed an analysis of the real character of the capitalist mode of production on the basis of a general theory of history as a process of struggle between classes. By means of this analysis they were able to outline the tendencies inherent in capitalism that drove it towards its overthrow by the conscious action of the proletariat it had created. This theme remains present from *The German Ideology* to *The Critique of the Gotha Programme*.

Yet their assertion of the scientific character of historical materialism gave rise to a typically philosophical problem. Wherein lies the scientificity of Marxism? To provide a reply to this question seemed to require two things. Firstly, it required a general theory of the

10

sciences and their relation to reality in order to provide an objective foundation for the claim that Marxism is a science. That is, it seemed to require a theory that could determine the validity of Marxism's claim to provide objective knowledge of the real world – an epistemology. Secondly, it required an identification of those specific features of Marxist theory from which its scientific character derived. Marx and Engels had always rejected the version of empiricism that rests the scientificity of a theory upon the immediate correspondence of the theory and the facts, since facts are themselves theoretical constructs.[3] Therefore the scientific character of Marxism must involve crucially the structure of the theory itself. And this is of course the answer Marxists have unanimously given: the dialectic, the form the theory takes in reflecting the relations in which social formations consist, is what makes Marxism a scientific theory.

This problem, the problem of the dialectic, is not simply of theoretical relevance: how it is settled has tremendous political implications. For, it embraces what has come to be known as the problem of the superstructure. The first sentence of the Marxist ABC states that in the final analysis it is the productive process that determines the character of, and modes of development open to, a social formation. But the question immediately arises, what role does the superstructure, i.e. the state apparatus, the ideological formations, etc. specific to that social formation, play? Is it strictly determined by the economy, or does it possess a certain autonomy, and if so, how much autonomy? This is obviously a matter of great political significance. For, if the superstructure is simply a reflex of the productive process, then the socialist revolution does not require the active intervention of revolutionaries, but can be achieved thanks to the automatism of the economy. If, on the other hand, political and ideological factors are (relatively) autonomous, then the need for conscious organisation and preparation is clear-cut.

The resolution of this question involves an understanding of the Marxist dialectic. For, as Lukacs was the first to point out, the category of totality is the decisive category of Marxist philosophy.[4] Marxism conceives of each social formation as a whole, as a structure which determines the nature and role of each of its parts. The solution

11

to the problem of the superstructure, therefore, depends on the way in which we see this whole. We shall see that Marxist philosophy has presented us with more than one notion of totality. It is into this question, that of the nature of the social whole in Marxism, that the problem of the materialist dialectic resolves itself.

It was, however, rather the first problem that I mentioned, the problem of providing Marxism with a general epistemological foundation, which exercised Engels. His solution can be found in *Anti-Dühring* and the posthumous *Dialectics of Nature*. It lay, essentially, in interpreting the dialectic not simply as providing the structures specific to Marx's analyses of social formations like capitalism, but as actually representing the laws immanent in all reality, natural as well as social, and in its reflection in thought.

Historical materialism became a specification of the general laws of reality, expounded by dialectical materialism. For this metaphysical *tour de force* there was, of course, a precedent. Hegel's avowedly idealistic dialectic involved a similar erection of the laws of the dialectic into laws informing every aspect of reality. Indeed Engels took directly from Hegel's *Science of Logic* the three main laws of the materialist dialectic:

> the law of the transformation of quantity into quality and vice versa;
> the law of the interpenetration of opposites;
> the law of the negation of the negation;[5]

Engels (and he was not the last Marxist to do so) was playing with philosophical fire. The categories of Hegel's dialectic carry with them a specific theoretical meaning that derives directly from the nature of his system. For Hegel the dialectic is the process through which Being, independent of all determinations, undergoes a metamorphosis that takes it through the stages of Logic, Nature and Spirit to the moment of Absolute Knowledge when the whole of reality is grasped by Absolute Spirit as its own manifestation. All previous idealist philosophers (with the partial exception of Spinoza) had separated Spirit (God) from the material world, asserting the supremacy of the former over the latter; Hegel sought to achieve the same goal by developing the *process* through which Spirit and the material world were *united*. The laws of the dialectic of which Engels writes, above all the negation of the negation (of which more below), form the mechanism through which everything is transformed into an emanation of Spirit.

Engels's solution to this problem is well known. He drew a distinction between Hegel's idealist system and his dialectical method and argued that Marx's theoretical revolution lay in rejecting the system but adopting the method, treating it not as the progress of the Absolute through the world and through history, but as a means of analysing the world. This is the famous setting of Hegel on his feet.[6] The same type of metaphorical language is employed by Marx in the celebrated Afterword to the Second German Edition of *Capital*, Volume I. As we shall see, a critique of the ambiguities inherent in this approach is the starting point for Althusser's own account of the dialectic.

For Engels, then, the dialectical laws Hegel had discovered were the general laws governing nature, history and thought. Marx's work was the triumphant application of these laws to history. Engels believed, moreover, that certain of the greater results of nineteenth-century natural science confirmed the interconnected and dialectical character of nature itself: the formulation of the general principle of conservation of energy, the discovery of the organic cell, and Darwin's theory of evolution.[7] The great epistemological problem of the relation between thought and reality was easily resolved:

> The fact that our subjective thought and the objective world are subject to the same laws, and, hence, too, that in the final analysis they cannot contradict each other in their results, but must coincide, governs absolutely our whole theoretical thought. It is the unconscious and unconditional premiss for theoretical thought.[8]

The common structure of both thought and the world guarantees their ultimate correspondence.

Thus, in Engels's hands, Marxist philosophy became a general philosophy of nature.[9] The political effects of this position became clear in the next generation of Marxists for whom Engels's philosophy, above all *Anti-Dühring*, was the orthodoxy. And it was they —

Kautsky, Plekhanov, etc. – who were to provide the leadership of the Second International. In their hands, Marxism itself was gradually transformed into a deterministic metaphysic which served both to justify their day-to-day reformist practice and to guarantee the arrival (one day) of the goal their practice was allegedly intended to reach, proletarian revolution.[10]

It is worth noting the extent to which the major debates in the Second International centred around the problem of the superstructure. For Kautsky, the laws developed by Marx in *Capital* were natural laws which governed not only the economy but also the superstructure, as the economy's ideological and political reflex. Thus:

> Capitalist society has failed; its dissolution is only a question of time; irresistible economic development leads with natural necessity to the bankruptcy of the capitalist mode of production. The erection of a new form of society in place of the existing one is no longer merely *desirable*; it has become something *inevitable*.[11]

Marxists were thereby absolved from the task of organising and intervening in the class struggle to win the leadership of the proletariat in the revolutionary cause: the laws of development of the capitalist mode of production would inevitably lead to socialism. Hilferding and the Austro-Marxists did not question the deterministic character of the laws of historical materialism; they argued rather that they were scientific and economic laws which could provide no justification for political action to overthrow capitalism: under the influence of neo-Kantian positivism they argued for the supplementation of Marxism with a socialist ethic. Thus, Hilferding wrote:

> It is . . . incorrect . . . simply to identify Marxism and socialism. Considered logically, as a scientific system alone . . . Marxism is only a theory of the laws of motion of society. . . . To recognise the validity of Marxism (which implies the recognition of the necessity of socialism) is by no means a task for value judgements, let alone a pointer to a practical line of conduct. It is one thing to recognise a necessity, but quite another to place oneself at the service of that necessity.[12]

Bernstein, as the leading revisionist, did not reject the terms of the debate; rather, he denied the correctness of Marx's theory as an analysis of capitalism and therefore called for its revision, and, again under the influence of positivism, for the supplementation of the 'purely factual' laws of historical materialism with the value judgements of a socialist ethics.

The absence of an articulated scientific theory of the superstructure was the theoretical condition for this mystified debate (there were, of course, other, material and political, conditions). A proper understanding that Marxism was not simply or even at all an economic theory but rather a theory of the social totality, and of the relations existing between the economy and the other instances of the whole, would have undercut the entire debate. Even the concept of the economy in Marx is the concept of an essentially social and historical entity, the unity of the *social* relations of production and the productive forces, rather than that of the technological conditions of material production.

Thus, in *Capital*, Volume I, Marx shows how the *technological* development of the productive forces, rather than providing the motor for the growth of capitalism was a *result* of the emergence of capitalist social relations of production – the separation of the direct producer from the means of production, the consequent transformation of labour power into a commodity, and the concentration of the means of production in the hands of the buyer of labour power, the capitalist – which required that production's narrow technical base be revolutionised.

But Marx's scientific work had concentrated on the economic instance of the capitalist mode of production, and, although important pointers for a theory of the superstructure exist both in *Capital* and in Marx's political writings, they are not in any more clearly articulated form that which Althusser would call 'the practical state'. Engels obliquely recognised this lacuna towards the end of his life in those passages in his correspondence where he criticises those who did not recognise the relative autonomy of the political and the fact that the economy was determinant only in the last instance.[13] These assertions, however, although instructive, were no substitute for a theory.

For the Marxists of the Second International, above all Kautsky, capitalism would inevitably, by 'natural necessity' be

15

replaced by socialism. This theoretical position provided a perfect cover for the fracture running deep through their politics – the fracture between the workers' movement and its goal, state power, between the social-democratic parties' increasingly reformistic practice and their revolutionary programmes, between their immediate tactics and a strategy aimed at workers' power. The expanding capitalism of imperialism's zenith before 1914 provided the space within which mass reformist parties could be built under the banner of revolutionary Marxism without any embarrassing conflict between theory and practice. Bernstein's revisionism was little more than impatience with a revolutionary rhetoric that did not fit the reformist reality of the Second International. It required the crisis of 1914, which forced the Marxists of Europe to choose between their own capitalist states and the international workers' movement, for the fracture to become a fissure dividing revolution from reform.

Hegelian Marxism

The political crisis brought with it a philosophical crisis. For it was clear that the mechanistic treatment of Marxism by Kautsky and others had served to transform it into a rhetorical mask for their reformist practice in the face of capitalism's greatest crisis. It was therefore necessary to think the political crisis in philosophy and to effect the necessary theoretical reinterpretation of Marxism which could both capture its critical and scientific character and account for the role which ideological and political factors play in determining whether a crisis can become a revolution.[14]

Common to all those who contributed to this renaissance was a return to Hegel. The most important case was, of course, that of Lenin, who, during the first two years of the war, studied Hegel's works, above all *The Science of Logic*, and came to the celebrated conclusion:

> *Aphorism:* It is impossible completely to understand Marx's *Capital*, and especially its first chapter, without having thoroughly understood the *whole* of Hegel's *Logic*. Consequently, half a century later none of the Marxists understood Marx.[15]

Some of the revolts against the fatalistic Marxism of the Second International took an extreme form: thus Gramsci, who had been greatly influenced by the idealist philosophers Croce and Bergson, wrote a famous article in *Avanti* after the October revolution entitled *The Revolution against 'Capital'* in which he celebrated the Bolsheviks as having restored the revolutionary essence of Marxism, against the deterministic laws of *Capital*. The most important figures of the period were Gramsci himself, Karl Korsch and, above all, Georg Lukacs, whose *History and Class Consciousness* remains the key text for the Hegelian Marxism of this group.[16]

The Hegelians (as I will call them from now on) broke with the determinism of the Second International by placing at the centre of their philosophical discussions the question of the relation between consciousness and reality. This question embraced two problems. The first was that of the relation between theory and practice. More concretely, how could Marxists move from a scientific critique of capitalism to the practice that would win the proletariat to support its overthrow? What were the theoretical conditions inherent in Marxism that would enable it to overcome the ideological hold the bourgeoisie enjoys over the working class through its control over the production and dissemination of ideas? The second was the epistemological problem of the relation between a science and the reality it seeks to explain and of the justification of a particular theory's claim to provide a knowledge of reality.

The identification of these two problems is validated by a problematic which derives from Hegel, and which Althusser calls historicism. A theory possesses a claim to cognitive validity to the extent that it is appropriate to the historical needs of a particular class in a particular epoch. Such a theory serves not only to provide the class with an understanding of reality sufficient for its needs, but also serves as an instrument in the assertion of its claim to dominate society, as a means of exercising its ideological and political, as well as economic, control over other classes and social groups. Marxism is scientific, therefore, because it serves the needs of the proletariat in its struggle for power. There is, indeed, a qualitative difference between Marxism and the theories of preceding classes, but this derives from the fact that the proletariat will, if it gains state power, be able to abolish not merely capitalism, but with it all class society, and to replace it with a classless communist society. Thus Marxism and the other sciences are ideologies, parts of the superstructure, whose validity depends on the changing course of history.

This means that Marxism's scientific validity consists in the historical function it performs in articulating the proletariat's will to power. The sciences do not derive their epistemological status from the construction of theories in order to explain reality but from their role in the formation of the world views of particular social classes.

How this is worked out varies according to the thinker. In the case of Gramsci, it is closely tied up with his theory of hegemony, of the mechanisms whereby the ruling class ensures its ideological and political control over society and hence of the problems a Marxist party would face in seeking to win the masses to its side. A class conception of the world, the ideology appropriate to its situation, both actual and potential, is implicit in its practice:

> The active man-in-the-mass has a practical activity, but has no clear theoretical consciousness of his practical activity, which nonetheless involves understanding the world insofar as it transforms it. His theoretical consciousness can indeed be historically in opposition to his activity. One might almost say that he has two theoretical consciousnesses (or one contradictory consciousness): one which is implicit in his activity and which in reality unites him with all his fellow workers in the practical transformation of the real world; and one, superficially explicit or verbal, which he has inherited from the past and uncritically absorbed.[17]

The role of the revolutionary party is to articulate and act upon the conception of the world implicit in the practice of the proletariat on the basis of a theory,

> which, by coinciding and identifying itself with the decisive elements of the practice itself, can accelerate the historical process that is going on, rendering practice more homogeneous, more coherent, more efficient in all its elements, and thus, in other words, developing its potential to the maximum.[18]

And the criterion of scientificity of a theory is the extent to which it articulates the practice of the class whose conception of the world it is;

18

this can be tested by the success that attempts to win support from the masses for the theory have: 'Mass adhesion or non-adhesion to an ideology is the real critical test of the rationality and historicity of modes of thinking.'[19]

Lukacs's work, on the other hand, is dominated by his pre-occupation with classical bourgeois philosophy, and he saw Marxism as the resolution of the latter's contradictions. From Galileo and Descartes onwards, the great bourgeois philosophers had set themselves the aim of arriving at a rational and comprehensive understanding of reality.

> But reality can only be understood and penetrated as a totality, and only a subject which is itself a totality is capable of this penetration. It was not for nothing that the young Hegel erected his philosophy on the principle that 'truth must be understood and expressed not merely as substance but also as subject'.[20]

An object which is completely separate from and alien to the subject which seeks to know it is incomprehensible: for it to be known there must exist an underlying unity between the object and the subject such that the subject can see the object as its creation. This 'grandiose conception that thought can only grasp what it has itself created',[21] the principle of the *identity of subject and object*, lies at the heart of bourgeois philosophy. But to comprehend the world requires more than seeing it as an emanation of the subject that seeks to know it. Reality must be seen *as a totality*. The alternative would be to remain a captive of the immediate appearance of things, seeing the world as a chaos of discrete facts possessing no comprehensible objective structure. Thus Hume's scepticism was the inevitable result of British philosophy's empiricism. 'To leave empirical reality behind can only mean that the objects of the empirical world are to be understood as aspects of a totality, i.e. as the aspects of a total social situation caught up in the process of historical change.'[22] To capture the meaning of the stream of events that present themselves to our consciousness requires an understanding of how they arose and developed as part of a social whole.

Yet to see the world as a totality is impossible for bourgeois philosophy. The maximum to which it can attain is to subsume some

19

particular sector of reality under rational laws; but any grasp of the whole is denied it. Thus Kant was able to provide a philosophical foundation for the laws of Newtonian mechanics not as the laws governing reality but as the structure of the appearances of the natural world and this only as a result of treating these principles as part of the conceptual mechanism necessary for a human subject to be conscious of the impressions it receives. But any understanding of reality as a whole is denied man and consigned to the realm of unknowable things-in-themselves. Only Hegel was able to systematically think the world as a totality resting upon the identity of the knowing subject and known object. But at what a price: the world of nature and of men was reduced to an epiphenomenon of the Absolute Idea, whose realisation lay in the dialectical process in which the Notion emerged in thought, became alienated from itself in the static world of nature and finally became conscious of itself in human history. The point of self knowledge, of the complete identity of subject and object, was reached in the mind of the philosopher when he recognised the world as the emanation of the Idea. And this recognition came only *post festum*: history was understood only when it was completed:

> As the thought of the world, it [philosophy – AC] appears only when actuality is already there cut and dried after its process of formation has been completed. The teaching of the concept, which is also history's inescapable lesson, is that it is only when actuality is nature that the ideal first appears over against the real and that the ideal apprehends this same real world in its substance and builds it up for itself into the shape of an intellectual realm. When philosophy paints its grey in grey it cannot be rejuvenated but only understood. The owl of Minerva spreads its wings only with the falling of the dusk.[23]

The tragic contradiction at the heart of classical philosophy reflected the basic contradiction of capitalism. That is, the contradiction between the extent to which the bourgeoisie can impose upon particular aspects of society a structure which is rational and therefore amenable to control, and its inability to control the system as a whole. Society is seen as an aggregation of discrete things, bound together by the relations of the market rather than by any sort of conscious control. This reified structure both masks and reflects the real social relations underlying it, the transformation of the worker into a thing through the purchase and sale of his labour power as a commodity.

> This rationalisation of the world seems to be complete, it seems to penetrate the very depth of man's physical and psychic nature. It is limited, however, by its own formalism. That is to say, the rationalisation of isolated aspects of life results in the creation of – formal – laws. All these things join together into what seems to the superficial observer to constitute a unified system of 'general' laws. But the disregard of the concrete aspects of the subject matter of these laws, upon which disregard their authority as laws is based, makes itself felt in the incoherence of the system in fact. This incoherence becomes particularly egregious in periods of crisis.[24]

Reification – the transformation of relations between men into a collection of discrete things, rendering possible a detailed control over parts of society and nature at the price of an inability to comprehend and master the whole – is reflected throughout society, not only at the economic level – despotism in the factory, anarchy in the market – but at the political and ideological levels. Hence the crisis of classical philosophy.

Only the proletariat can offer a way out. For only the proletariat, through its practice, can attain in reality the identity of subject and object which Hegel was able to realise only in a speculative and mystified form. This is a result of the reduction of the worker to a commodity.

> The worker can only become conscious of his existence in society when he becomes aware of himself as a commodity. As we have seen, his immediate existence integrates him as a pure, naked object into the production process. Once this immediacy turns out to be the consequence of a multiplicity of mediations, once it becomes evident how much it presupposes, then the fetishistic forms of the commodity system begin to dissolve: in the commodity the worker recognises himself and his own relations with capital. Inasmuch as he is incapable in practice of raising himself above the role of object his consciousness is the *self-consciousness of the commodity*; or in other words it is the self-revelation of the capitalist society founded upon the production and exchange of commodities.[25]

21

The position of the working class drives it towards an attempt to understand society as a totality, an understanding which it, unlike the bourgeoisie, can achieve because of its objective interest in the abolition of capitalism. Indeed the class consciousness of the proletariat is its most powerful advantage in its struggle for power.

> The proletariat cannot liberate itself as a class without simultaneously abolishing class society as such. For that reason its consciousness, the last class consciousness in the history of mankind, must both lay bare the nature of society and achieve an increasingly inward fusion of theory and practice. 'Ideology' for the proletariat is no banner to follow into battle, nor is it a cover for its true objectives: it is the objective and weapon itself.[26]

Of course, the proletariat as a whole, or at least sections within it, may not reach the class consciousness appropriate to its position. The necessity for a revolutionary party derives from this fact; its possibility is a result of the fact that it is possible to ascribe to a class the consciousness appropriate to its position: 'class consciousness consists in fact of the appropriate and rational reactions "imputed" to a particular typical position in the process of production.'[27] The party represents this imputed class consciousness of the proletariat, transcending the contingent failures of the class to arrive at full consciousness.

The strengths of Gramsci's and Lukacs's positions reflect each thinker's particular achievements – Gramsci's marvellously acute analyses of the ideological and political preconditions of revolution, Lukacs's deep understanding of classical German philosophy. However, both their common positions and the detailed fashion in which each respective position is worked out rest upon a fundamental error.

The identification of which I spoke in introducing their work – of the problem of the unity of theory and practice and the problem of the relation between science and its object is an invalid and illicit conflation of questions of quite a different order. The first problem is the fundamental problem of Marxist politics: how to give ideas a material force, as Marx put it, by transcending the separation between the in-

22

tellectual workers who have produced a scientific knowledge of capitalism and the possibilities of its overthrow, and the masses upon whose action this overthrow depends and who will rule the society which follows it. This is the problem of *What is to be Done?* and the whole of Lenin's work reflects a deep understanding of the problem. The second problem is the epistemological one: how to guarantee that a theory does in fact provide a knowledge of the reality it claims to explain. To conflate the two problems is possible within the Hegelian problematic because, for Hegel, philosophy rested upon the abolition of the distinction between thought and being and the assertion of their identity. The problem of the epistemological relation between thought and reality could slide into that of how to make thought reality because for Hegel thought *was* the real. And here is the great problem for Marxist philosophy: how can we assert that Marxism is dialectical when the dialectic, in Hegel's hands at least (and neither of the major traditions in Marxist philosophy has rejected Hegel's basic categories), is idealist through and through? For Lukacs, Gramsci and Korsch this is not a problem. I shall attempt to show the difficulties this creates.

To take Gramsci first. Although less explicitly than in Lukacs's case, his philosophy rests upon the identity of subject and object. Thus. 'Our knowledge of things is nothing other than ourselves, our needs and our interests.'[28] Therefore he denies any sharp separation between thought and the reality it seeks to know. Marxist theory renders explicit what is implicit in the practice of the proletariat, thus providing the theoretical answer to the problems posed to us by history whose solution lies in the proletarian revolution:

> If [Marx] has analysed reality exactly then he has done nothing other than systematise rationally and coherently what the historical agents of this reality felt and feel still in a confused and instinctive way, and of which they have a clearer consciousness as a result of the hostile critique.[29].

This denial of a sharp separation between thought and reality goes hand in hand with a denial that beyond the appearances, beyond the immediate needs and activities of men, there is any underlying

23

structure which is responsible for the way in which things present themselves. Rather, the real is a historical goal, to be attained as a result of the creation of a communist society:

> Man knows objectively in so far as knowledge is real for the whole human race *historically* unified in a single unified cultural system. But this process of historical unification takes place through the disappearance of the internal contradictions which tear apart human society, while these contradictions themselves are the condition for the formation of groups and for the birth of ideologies which are not concretely universal but which are immediately rendered transient by the practical origin of their substance. There exists therefore a struggle for objectivity (to free oneself from partial and fallacious ideologies) and this struggle is the same as the struggle for the cultural unification of the human race.[30]

There exists a sharp contradiction between Gramsci's epistemology, which ultimately identifies objectivity with unanimity, and the conception of science present in Marx's work. For Marx, the objectivity of science is something that can be achieved, not as a historical result of proletarian revolution but through the work of the scientist. This is possible once the appearances are seen to be exactly that, appearances. The effort of science is therefore concentrated upon the attempt to grasp the mechanisms at work beneath the appearances responsible both for these appearances and for the workings of reality. In the case of historical materialism this is the function of the theory of fetishism, which rests upon the radical disjunction between the way in which the capitalist mode of production appears – as the sum of the market relations between commodities – and the underlying social relations of exploitation that generate this mystified appearance. In this, historical materialism differs sharply from vulgar economy, whose latest embodiment is neo-classical economics:

> Vulgar economy actually does no more than interpret, systematise and defend in doctrinaire fashion the conceptions of the agents of bourgeois production who are entrapped in bourgeois production relations. It should not astonish us, then, that vulgar economy feels particularly at home in the estranged outward appearances of economic relations in which these *prima facie* absurd and perfect con-

tradictions appear, and that these relations seem the more self-evident the more their internal relationships are concealed from it, although they are understandable to the popular mind. But all science would be superfluous if the outward appearance and the essence of things directly coincided.[31]

Thus the objectivity of science is a reality, not a regulative principle that points towards a future goal, a reality rendered possible by the disjunction between the appearances and the real relations underlying them. Yet, since Gramsci denies the existence of any reality beyond the immediate needs and activities of men, he has no choice but to ground the objectivity of science upon a historical teleology.

Moreover, Marx asserts a sharp separation between thought and reality. Indeed, the existence of the sciences presupposes their separation from reality.

The totality as it appears in the head, as a totality of thoughts, is a product of a thinking head, which appropriates the world in the only way that it can, a way different from the artistic, religious, practical and mental appropriation of the world. The real subject retains its autonomous existence outside the head just as before; namely as long as the head's conduct is merely speculative, merely theoretical. Hence, in the theoretical method, too, the subject, society, must always be kept in mind as the presupposition.[32]

Marx's materialism is based upon the assertion of the *primacy of being over thought*, and at the same time upon their *separation*, thought as a reflection of reality. But, to this we shall return.[33]

A further consequence of Marx's theory of the sciences radically contradicts Gramsci's epistemology. For, as can be seen from the passage about vulgar economy quoted above, the agents of capitalist production, worker and capitalist alike are 'entrapped' by the mystified way in which the relations of production appear. Yet another quotation will back this up:

If . . . the analysis of the actual intrinsic relations of the capitalist process of production is a very complicated matter and very extensive; if it is a work of science to resolve the visible, merely external movement into the true intrinsic movement, it is self-evident that conceptions which arise about the laws of production in the minds of the agents of capitalist mode of production and circulation will diverge drastically from these real laws and will merely be the conscious expression of the visible movements.[34]

Marx makes it clear that this is a *necessity* for the capitalist mode of production: built into its operation is the mystified way in which it presents itself to the agents of production, capitalist and worker alike. Yet if the practice of the worker in the capitalist productive process is necessarily impregnated with bourgeois ideology, then the foundation for Gramsci's epistemology collapses. For how can Marxism perform the function of rendering explicit what is implicit in the practice of the proletariat if that practice is, spontaneously at least, *necessarily mystified*? Clearly an alternative account of the status of historical materialism and its relation to the working class is required. To this also we shall return.[35]

If Gramsci's epistemology leads to serious philosophical difficulties, it does not, in itself, lead to any major political errors. The dominant element in Gramsci's theory is not his philosophical position but his analysis of the role of ideologies and the state, which is incomparable and indeed impregnates his philosophy, as I have already pointed out. The same cannot be said of Lukacs, in whose work the philosophical element is dominant. The best characterisation of Lukacs's philosophy as outlined in *History and Class Consciousness* is that it is an attempt to resolve the contradictions of bourgeois philosophy *from within the problematic of bourgeois philosophy itself.* The master category Lukacs employs is that of the *subject* and the key to a resolution of the problems of bourgeois philosophy lies in the correct employment of this category: a scientific understanding of reality can be attained only through the identity of subject and object. Knowledge is self-knowledge. Only the proletariat can achieve the identity of subject and object since, paradoxically, their degradation to the status of things, commodities, enables them to grasp the essence of the reifications of capitalist society, the commodity-structure at its heart. 'Historical materialism in its classical form . . . means *the self-knowledge of capitalist society*.'[36]

Yet I doubt whether this solution is internally coherent. For

Marx makes it very clear that the proletariat is the result, the creation, of capitalism. The Hegelian problematic in which Lukacs is operating requires the subject to see the object as its creation. This cannot be so with the proletariat: it is not its own creator. Indeed in *Capital* there is no creator of the proletariat: it is, rather, the *result* of a *process*, firstly, the process of primitive accumulation whereby the preconditions for capitalist production are created, and secondly the actual process of capitalist accumulation itself, which indeed rests upon the workers as the source of value but cannot be reduced to them. Hence the proletariat is disqualified from playing the role of identical subject-object, and Lukacs's system collapses.[37]

Even if we were prepared to accept Lukacs's position as coherent, there are its political consequences, which are extremely serious. For Lukacs, the decisive political struggle is fought out at the level of consciousness:

> When confronted by the overwhelming resources of knowledge, culture and routine which the bourgeoisie undoubtedly possesses and will continue to possess so long as it remains the ruling class, the only effective superiority of the proletariat, its only decisive weapon, is its ability to see the social totality as a concrete historical totality; to see the reified forms as processes between men, to see the immanent meaning of history that only appears negatively in the contradictions of abstract forms, to raise its positive side to consciousness and to put it into practice.[38]

Now, of course, it is true that it is only when the working class becomes conscious of its position in the capitalist mode of production and of the ability this position gives it to seize political power and abolish the conditions of oppression and exploitation that characterise all previous class societies, that proletarian revolution can become an actuality. But it is not the class consciousness of the proletariat that is its decisive weapon. Rather, it is the unique position that the working class possesses under capitalism as the producer of value in conditions which continually tend to create a socially cohesive and united class, on the one hand, and which, on the other, develop the productive forces to the point where capitalism and, indeed, any other form of exploitation, is unnecessary and thus drive the system towards crisis.[39]

27

Moreover, to make the decisive struggle that at the ideological level is to abstract from the class struggle's stake: political power. It is therefore to abstract from the conditions under which the proletariat can seize power and from the necessity for the proletariat to smash the bourgeois state apparatus and replace it with a regime of workers' councils.

Finally, Lukacs's analysis, when it comes to the question of how the working class breaks with bourgeois ideology and develops its own class consciousness, is very poor. To treat the revolutionary party as the reflex of the class consciousness of the proletariat is to do two things. Firstly, it is to evade the real problems that Lenin, Trotsky and Gramsci grappled with – the problems of building a party that combines a scientific analysis of capitalism with real roots in the working class, and of winning to the side of that party a majority of the working class and of the other oppressed sections whose interests lie in the direction of proletarian revolution – to evade, that is, the problem of hegemony. Secondly, it is to provide the theoretical basis for an ultra-leftism that sees the action of the vanguard in terms of what the class ought to think, rather than adapting its tactics to what the class actually does think in order to intervene to transform the consciousness of the class in the direction of revolutionary Marxism. The conception of the party present in *History and Class Consciousness* is the foundation for the ultra left line that Lukacs took in the Third International in the early twenties, in opposition to the line of Lenin and Trotsky, who argued for the deepest involvement in the class in order to win over a majority, including work in the trade unions, participation in bourgeois elections and united fronts with reformist parties.[40] We can see that Lukacs's employment of the category of the subject to solve the political and epistemological problems faced by Marxism led him to serious political errors.[41]

Despite the much greater sophistication of the Hegelian position it did not succeed in replacing the orthodoxy deriving from Engels. Lukacs and Korsch were bitterly attacked as idealists by Zinoviev at the Fifth Congress of the Comintern in 1924. Bukharin, as one of the leading Bolshevik theoriticians, wrote a general treatise on Marxism, *Historical Materialism*, which represented a restatement of the orthodox tradition in the form of an extreme technological determinism. It was not by chance that this work was singled out for attack by both Lukacs and Gramsci.[42] But with the triumph of Stalin in the Bolshevik Party, and the subsequent subordination of the Comintern to the CPSU, the 'orthodox' position was transformed into holy writ. This transformation culminated in the vulgar evolutionism of Stalin's *Dialectical and Historical Materialism*, a chapter in the notorious *Short Course in the History of the CPSU (b)*, and the consecration of Stalin's massacre of the old Bolsheviks during the purges of the thirties.[43]

The current revival of interest in the great Hegelians of the 1910s and 1920s coincided with the crisis of post-war Stalinism, to which I have already referred. Just as in the early decades of this century this revival is a political phenomenon. For, during the 1960s and early 1970s it became clear that the post-war stabilisation of capitalism was coming to an end. Imperialism was facing a fundamental challenge, not only on its frontiers in the Third World, in Algeria and Indochina and Southern Africa, where wars of national liberation broke out, but also in its heartlands, as massive social struggles broke out in which increasingly the industrial working class was the protagonist: in France in May 1968, in Italy in the autumn of 1969, in Britain from the late 1960s, in Portugal today. Once again there re-emerge the problems that had driven Lenin and Gramsci, Lukacs and Korsch, to philosophy, to think through the ideological and political problems that the opening of the capitalist system to revolutionary overthrow give rise to. Once again the problem of the relation between the economy and the superstructure, the problems of a revolutionary political practice that can win a majority of the working class to the cause of proletarian revolution, came to the fore. In the continued absence of a theory of the superstructure, philosophy once more came to carry the burden. We shall now turn, at last, to Althusser's attempt to meet the demands that revolutionary practice today makes on Marxist philosophy.

2. The System

Readings and Problematics

One of the chief stimuli to the revival of interest in Marxist philosophy was the discovery and publication of two major theoretical works by Marx that had been hitherto unknown. The first was a work known as the *Economic and Philosophical Manuscripts*, which first appeared in 1931. It represents Marx's earliest encounter with political economy and was written by him after his conversion to revolutionary communism while staying in Paris in 1843–44. The structure of the manuscripts is thoroughly Hegelian. The object of political economy is the condition of man under capitalism, a condition in which man is separated from his life activity, his labour, controlled as it is not by him but by the capitalist and subordinated to the end of satiating the capitalist's greed rather than fulfilling man's real needs. This condition is a necessary result of the interaction between man and nature: man affirms his essence by transforming nature through his labour, but nature also transforms him by changing him into a mere object separated from his species being, labour. However, this condition of alienation is a necessary stage in the process of making man truly human: its goal is communism, the reconciliation of man's existence with his essence through the abolition of the alienated labour that exists under capitalism. As we can see, an inversion of the Hegelian dialectic has taken place: rather than the Absolute Idea, the subject of the dialectic is man's essence. The structure of the dialectic, however, is the same. In both cases the process is teleological, moving towards a predetermined end: the alienation of the subject, in Hegel's case in nature, in Marx's in capitalism, is a necessary stage in its fuller realisation, and the process is governed by the necessity of the attainment of the goal. What makes the process dialectical in both cases is the fact that the goal is *immanent* in the process; rather than existing at a point external to the process of attaining to it the goal necessarily arises and is attained within the process.[1]

The other text, the *Grundrisse*, first published in 1939–40, consists of Marx's notebooks on political economy, written in 1857–58. They can be seen as the first stage in the writing of *Capital*. In themselves they are, very largely, an attempt by Marx to think out the problems of classical political economy from the standpoint of historical materialism and, as such, contain important if uneven results.[2] Their philosophical significance rests on a number of passages which have been interpreted as reflecting a continuity between this work and the *Manuscripts* of 1844.

These works, particularly the *Manuscripts*, have been claimed by Hegelian Marxists as a confirmation of their version of the materialist dialectic. The *Manuscripts* had a tremendous influence upon Lukacs, who attempted to recast the whole of the philosophical position introduced in *History and Class Consciousness* so as to base it upon the interaction between man and nature in the labour process.[3] It was argued that the foundation for Marx's later political and economic analysis was laid in the ontology of the *Manuscripts*, the idea of man as a self-creating being arising out of the dialectic between his labour and the natural world it transformed.[4] Here we see at work the problematic common to almost all Marxist philosophical positions: the attempt to give the source of historical materialism a philosophical foundation outside itself, whether in the dialectics of nature, or the dialectic between subject and object (of which the dialectic between labour and nature is a special case). We shall have occasion to return to this problematic below.

Althusser's work commences with a critique of this, the humanist, interpretation of Marx. He argued that it rested upon an empiricist epistemology according to which the meaning of a text is immediately accessible – the text need only be read to be understood. Thus, if the term 'alienation' is encountered both in the *Manuscripts* and in *Capital*, it follows that the concepts to which the term refers in both texts are the same. This is not, according to Althusser, simply a lack of scholarly rigour on the part of the Hegelian Marxists, a failure on their part to back up their claims by any sort of detailed investigation that establishes rather than asserts the identity of meaning of the term 'alienation' in the two texts.[5] It is also a special case of a theory of knowledge characteristic of bourgeois philosophy since at least Galileo, which involves a certain *theory of reading*.

According to this epistemology, the real is immediately present in the phenomena accessible to our observation. To grasp the real requires only a properly informed gaze, a gaze which can distinguish between the essence and its phenomena. This ability is guaranteed by an underlying complicity between subject and object – the structure of the object of knowledge is such as to render possible the penetration of the subject's gaze through the contingent to the real:

> To treat nature or reality as a Book, in which, according to Galileo, is spoken the silent discourse of a language whose 'characters are triangles, circles and other geometrical figures', it was necessary to have a certain idea of *reading* which makes a written discourse the immediate transparency of the true, and the real the discourse of a voice.[6]

To this theory of knowledge, Althusser counterposes a position which, if it is to be held consistently, involves the rejection of any such complicity between subject and object. Indeed, he argues, there exists the sharpest possible separation between the real object, that is, the reality which the theory seeks to explain, and the thought-object, the theoretical system which makes up a science. Rather than there existing any direct relation between the real and thought objects, the development of theory takes place strictly at the level of the thought-object:

> Knowledge working on its 'object' . . . does not work on the *real* object but on the peculiar raw material which constitutes, in the strict sense of the term, its *'object' (of knowledge)* and which, even in the most rudimentary forms of knowledge is distinct from the *real object*. For that raw material is ever-already, in the strong sense Marx gives it in *Capital*, a *raw material*, i.e. matter already elaborated and transformed, precisely by the imposition of the complex (sensuous-technical-ideological) structure which constitutes it as an *object of knowledge*, however crude, which constitutes it as the object it will transform, whose *forms* it will change in the course of its development process in

order to produce knowledges which are constantly *transformed* but will always apply to its *object*, in the sense of the *object of knowledge*.[7]

The thought-object is for Althusser what the concepts of a science are set to work on, as opposed to what the science is to provide knowledge *of*, the real object. As we will see more clearly below in the section on *The Autonomy of Theory*, what he wants to do is to distinguish sharply between reality and the process by which we come to know reality. The thought-object is, if you like, the precondition of the latter process. It consists in the *pre-existing* concepts and theories which the science sets about to transform in order to provide a more rigorous knowledge of the real. For Althusser what matters in the sciences is how the concepts constituting a science are deployed in order to develop it. The emphasis is upon the sciences as a historical practice undergoing continual transformations. By contrast, for empiricism scientific knowledge is the result of a pre-established harmony between thought and reality that precedes the work of any scientist. On Althusser's model of the sciences, their relation to the real is one that is secured and deepened through their own development.

From this position there followed a new theory of reading. This involved, not a direct relation between reader and text, but rather a dialectic between the theory whose principles govern the reading, and the theory contained in the text. Thus, there can be no 'innocent reading', i.e. no reading that does not involve, at least implicitly, a theory which determines the character of the reading.[8] This immediately raises the question of the nature of Althusser's reading of Marx:

> We read *Capital* as philosophers . . . (We posed it the question of its *relation to its object*, hence both the question of its specificity of its *object*, and the specificity of its *relation* to that object, i.e. the question of the nature of the type of discourse set to work to handle this object, the question of scientific discourse. And since there can never be a definition without a difference, we posed *Capital* the question of the specific difference both of its object and of its discourse.[9]

Although written of his and his collaborators' work on *Capital*, this passage applies to all Althusser's writings on Marx.

The passage reintroduces us to problems which I described in the previous chapter as being central to Marxist philosophy: the problems of the novel and peculiar character of historical materialism, of the nature of the Marxist dialectic, and of the general epistemology in terms of which this dialectic can be validly called scientific. Althusser recognises this explicitly: a Marxist reading of Marx 'presupposes activating a minimum of provisional Marxist theoretical concepts bearing on the nature of theoretical formations and their history'. It follows

> That the precondition of a reading of Marx is a Marxist theory of the differential nature of theoretical formations and their history, that is a theory of epistemological history, which is Marxist philosophy itself; that this operation in itself constitutes an indispensible circle in which the application of Marxist theory to Marx himself appears to be the absolute precondition of an understanding of Marx and at the same time as the precondition even of the constitution and development of Marxist philosophy.[10]

Althusser adds 'so much is clear'! What is clear is that according to him for Marxist philosophy to exist it must already exist! What is less clear is whether this claim is a coherent one. But perhaps it is a matter of dialectics. We shall see.[11]

The most important of the 'provisional Marxist theoretical concepts bearing on the nature of theoretical formations and their history' is that of *problematic*. This notion in fact derives originally not from Althusser himself, but from the great philosopher of science, Gaston Bachelard, under whom he had worked.[12] On Althusser's theory of reading understanding a text presupposes identifying the theory at work in the text. Following Bachelard, he asserts that the identity of a theory lies not in any specific propositions which the theory involves, or in the intentions of the theory's author, but in its structure, at the level of the way in which the problems that it is the function of the theory to solve are posed. That is to say. it lies at the level of the theory's problematic, '*the objective internal reference system of its particular* themes, the system of *questions* commanding the *answers* given'.[13]

In Althusser's hands, the concept of a theory's problematic

becomes that of the underlying structure which renders possible the raising of certain questions in a particular form, while ruling out the raising of others. An understanding of a particular problem is a result not of the qualities of the particular reader of the text which enable him to see it for what it is, but rather of the problematic of the theory in which he is working.

> This introduces us to a fact peculiar to the very existence of science: it can only pose problems on the terrain and within the horizon of a definite theoretical structure, its problematic, and hence the absolute determination of *the forms in which all problems must be posed*, at any given moment in the science.
>
> This opens the way to an understanding of the determination of the *visible* as visible, and conjointly of the invisible, as invisible, and of the organic link binding the invisible to the visible. Any object or problem situated on the terrain and with the horizon, i.e. in the definite structured field of the theoretical problematic of a given theoretical discipline is visible.[14]

Thus a necessary concomitant of the problems that are opened up by a particular problematic are those whose existence is denied:

> The same connexion that defines the visible also defines the invisible as its shadowy obverse. It is the field of the problematic that defines and structures the invisible as the definite excluded, *excluded* from the field of visibility and defined as excluded by the existence and peculiar structure of the field of the problematic.[15]

The problematic of a theory is objective: it is not reducible to the beliefs of the author of the theory; it is extractible by means of a *symptomatic reading*. It is called symptomatic because the problematic of a theory is complex and contradictory, involving dislocations between different levels. These contradictions are reflected on the text's surface, as *symptoms* of a complex structure, in gaps, lapses, silences, absences, which are determined by the way in which the contradictory levels of the theory are articulated upon each other. A symptomatic reading 'divulges the undivulged event in the text it reads, and in the same movement relates it to a *different text*, present as a necessary absence of the first'.[16] Only a symptomatic reading, which starts from this necessary complexity of the text, can articulate the questions posed in its gaps.

This is all very obscure. Perhaps the genealogy of this approach will throw some light on the matter. Althusser's theory of symptomatic reading is heavily influenced by Freud, who detected in the errors, omissions and absurdities of the discourse of dream and every-day life the symptoms of the complex and hidden structure of the un-conscious. But the category of problematic can also be seen at work in the writing of *Capital* itself. The British political economists had dis-covered the law of value, and even, as Marx says in *Theories of Surplus Value*, discovered the origin of surplus value in the exploita-tion of the worker. Yet it was left to Marx to develop these insights as the basis of a revolutionary yet scientific analysis of capitalism's historical trajectory. Why? Engels's answer in his Preface to *Capital*, Volume II, seems, as Althusser points out, to involve reference to some notion akin to that of problematic: 'What they [i.e. the classical economists] had regarded as a *solution*, he considered a problem.'[17]

In *Theories of Surplus Value*, Marx stringently criticises those socialists like Hodgskin, who, in order to attack capitalism, merely take up the categories of political economy and exploit their contradic-tions, thus remaining within the problematic of classical bourgeois economics. He writes of the author of one radical pamphlet:

> The author . . . stands on Ricardian ground and is only consistent in stating one of the consequences inherent in the system itself and he ad-vances it in the interest of the working class against capital.
> 'For the rest, the author remains a captive of the economic categories as he finds them.'[18]

Marx himself, on the other hand, did two things. First of all, he conducted, in his economic studies, a symptomatic reading of the political economists. That is to say, by operating in a problematic other than that of bourgeois economics, namely that of historical materialism, he was able to seize on and pose the questions which even Smith and Ricardo were driven towards without being able to pose because of the contradictions inherent in political economy. This remark is characteristic of his method in *Theories of Surplus Value*:

'Mr. Mill is not quite clear about the *question* which he seeks to answer. We will therefore formulate *his* question briefly before we hear his answer.'[19] This is not a result of Marx's superior insight, but of the fact that he was working within a problematic that enabled him to understand the way in which the immanent logic of bourgeois economy forced certain problems upon it though not in a form that would have made them open to solution, since this would be to put into question the capitalist system.

This brings us to the second thing Marx did, which was to pose the two central problems of classical economy and to solve them: first, is the exchange between capital and labour an exception to the law of value? Secondly, capitals with different organic compositions yield profits at the same rate – does this not also contradict the law of value? It was the fact of working in a problematic different from that of bourgeois political economy that enabled Marx to pose these problems in a form amenable to solution. It was only by shifting to a new terrain, outside the prison of the given economic categories, that Marx was able to see and answer the questions that bourgeois economy could not.

The first result of Althusser's theory of reading is found in *For Marx*. There Althusser argues that between the *Manuscripts* of 1844 and Marx's later work there existed a radical break. This break represented a change in problematics, and since a problematic systematically determines the range of problems with which a theory can deal, the change was therefore a complete one. Moreover this break, which Althusser dates as taking place in 1845 and as being embodied in the *Theses on Feuerbach* and *The German Ideology*, was not simply a change of problematic: it was an *epistemological break* between a science and the ideology that had preceded it. What happened was that Marx rejected the anthropological problematic of the *Manuscripts*, which limited him to metaphysical reflection rather than scientific analysis. He did so by, in the words of the Sixth Thesis on Feuerbach, identifying the human nature which had been the subject of history in his early works with 'the ensemble of social relations' and then going on to construct concepts specifying the nature of these social relations. These concepts were the basic concepts of historical

37

materialism, above all those of the relations and forces of production, which make up the Marxist concept of the economy and the contradictions between which motor the historical process.

I shall go into Althusser's theory of science and ideology at length below. Suffice it to say here that the difference between a science and a theoretical ideology is at the level of the nature of their problematics. The manner in which problems are posed in an ideology is such as to render it impossible for a continuous deepening and development of the theory to take place, limiting the ideology to confirming its own presuppositions, which in the last instance pertain not to the theory itself but to the social reality external to it:

> In the theoretical mode of production of ideology (which is utterly different from the theoretical mode of production of science in this respect), the formulation of a *problem* is merely the theoretical expression of the conditions which allow a *solution* already produced outside the process of knowledge because imposed by certain extra-theoretical instances and exigencies (by religious, ethical, political or other 'interests') *to recognise itself* in an artifical problem manufactured to serve it both as a theoretical mirror and a practical justification.[20]

The problematic of a science according to Althusser is such as to render it possible for it to develop, deepening the knowledges it produces, in a process of continual internal transformation, which at times will involve thoroughgoing recastings of the problematic such as the revolution in theoretical physics inaugurated by Einstein. An ideology is a closed system, while a science is essentially open to change from within.

Symptomatic readings such as Althusser's reading of Marx are rendered possible by historical materialism itself:

> *Capital* . . . exactly measures a distance and an internal dislocation in the real, inscribed in its *structure*, a distance and a dislocation such as to make their own effects themselves illegible, and the illusion of an immediate reading of them the ultimate apex of their effects: *fetishism* . . . Only from history in thought, the theory of history, was it possible to account for the historical religion of reading: by discovering that the truth of history cannot be read in its manifest discourse, because the

text of history is not a text in which a voice (the Logos) speaks, but the unaudible and illegible notation of the effects of a structure of structures.[21]

Althusser is here placing at the centre of Marx's science of history the theory of fetishism in *Capital*, which we will be looking at in the next section. Briefly, the theory stresses the necessary dislocation between the way in which the social whole operates and the way in which its operations are manifested. Thus, the complexity and opacity of the text is a special case of the complexity and opacity of history: only when a science that could decode the meaning of the historical process was elaborated could a theory of the nature of theoretical formations and the elusive meanings of the texts in which they are embodied arise. Here we have another example of the Althusserian circle: an understanding of Marxist theory can only be acquired by its application to itself. But let us leave that aside for the time being and take the cue Althusser offers us to turn to his discussion of the Marxist dialectic.

Overdetermination

Althusser's discussion of the dialectic begins with a rigorous critique of the metaphor of the inversion of Hegel's dialectic that Marx is alleged to have carried out. To suggest that the structure of the dialectic could remain the same while it was applied to completely different objects would imply a separation between the dialectic and its object hardly compatible with Hegel's assertion of the unity of the method of the dialectic and its object.[22] To alter the object of the dialectic would be to change its nature.

> This metaphorical expression – the 'inversion' of the dialectic – does not pose the problem of *the nature of the objects* to which a *single method* should be applied (the world of the Idea for Hegel – the real world for Marx) but rather the problem of the *nature of the dialectic* considered itself, that is, the problem of *its specific structures*; not the problem of the inversion of the 'sense' of the dialectic, but that of the *transformation of its structures*. It is hardly worth pointing out that, in the first case, the application of a method, the exteriority of the dialectic to its possible objects poses a *pre-dialectical question*, a question without any strict meaning for Marx.[23]

What, then, is common to both the Hegelian dialectic and the Marxist dialectic, which arises out of the transformation of the former's structures? Althusser's answer is that they share the basic conception of history as a process motored by the contradictions internal to it. The starting point for the differences between the two dialectics is therefore the different notions of contradiction they possess.

According to Althusser, in the Hegelian dialectic contradiction is *simple*. That is to say, all the instances of the totality reflect the basic contradiction. The Hegelian totality is an *expressive* totality, 'a totality all of whose parts are so many *'total parts'*, each expressing the others, and each expressing the social totality that contains them, because each in itself contains in the immediate form of its expression the essence of the totality itself'.[24] We encounter again the epistemology to which Althusser is attempting to offer an alternative: the totality is immediately present in, and extractible from, each of its parts. Each part of the whole is but the expression of the essence of the whole. Thus in Hegel's *Philosophy of History* the elements of each epoch are bound together in a totality 'which is *reflected in an unique internal principle*, which is *the truth* of all these concrete determinations'. The specificity of the elements is reduced to a moment in the self-development of the *Weltgeist*. History is a process moving towards a predetermined end, the rising of the Absolute to self-consciousness. As Althusser says of Hegel's *Phenomenology of Mind*:

> [The successive contradictions constitute] the complexity of a cumulative *internalisation* . . . at each moment of its development consciousness lives and experiences its own essence (the essence corresponding to the stage it has attained) *through all the echoes* of the essence it has previously been and through the *allusive presence* of the corresponding historical forms. . . . But these past *images* of consciousness and these latent *worlds* (corresponding to the images) never affect present consciousness as *effective determinations different from itself*: these images and worlds concern it only *as echoes* . . . of what it has become, that is, *as anticipations of or allusions to itself*. Because the past is never more than the internal essence (in-itself) of the future it encloses, this presence of the past is the presence to consciousness of consciousness to itself, *and no true external determination.*[25]

For Marx, history is not the expression of a spiritual essence, but a process whose development is the result of the relations of the distinct instances composing it; for, it is only on the basis of the irreducible distinctness of the parts of the whole that relations of determination, causal relations, rather than intimations of the Absolute, can be established. 'Where reality is concerned, we are never dealing with the pure existence of simplicity . . . but with the existence of "concretes" of complex and structured beings and processes.'[26] The complexity of the whole depends on the fact that it consists in a number of distinct but interrelated instances, apart from the economy itself – the political, the ideological, the theoretical – none of which are reducible to the economic.

The criticism that has been levelled at Althusser on this score by, among others, Roger Garaudy – that he has reduced Marxism to a theory of factors, to following the empirically diverse concatenations at different times of essentially separate and only contingently related factors – is enept. The complexity of the social totality possesses a structure – a *structure in dominance*. The contradiction within the economic between the social relations of production and the forces of production determines the character of the social totality because it determines which of the other instances is to be the dominant instance: thus, under feudalism, the political was the dominant instance, although, the economy was determinant in the last instance. Or, to put it another way, the determination of the economy consists precisely in assigning to a particular instance the role of dominant instance.[27] That the totality is structured is as essential to its nature as that it is complex:

> That one contradiction dominates the other presupposes that the complexity in which it features is a structured unity, and that this structure implies the indicated domination-subordination relations between the contradictions. . . . Domination is not just an indifferent *fact*, it is a fact *essential* to the complexity itself. That is why complexity implies domination as one of its essentials: it is inscribed in its structure. So to claim that this unity is not and cannot be the unity of a simple, original and universal essence is not . . . to sacrifice unity on the altar of 'pluralism' – it is to claim something quite different: that the unity discussed by Marxism is *the unity of the complexity itself*, that the mode of organisation and articulation of the complexity is precisely what con-

41

stitutes its unity. It is to claim that *the complex whole has the unity of a structure in dominance.*[28]

Now certain things follow from the complex unity of the social totality. I have already referred to the specificity of the instances of the totality, their distinctness and relative autonomy within the overall structure in dominance determined by the economy. To repeat, they are not an aggregation of essentially discrete factors. They possess a certain order, are organised into a certain hierarchy, according to the determination of the economy, which displaces the role of dominant instance onto a particular instance and allocates to the other instances their specific roles. However, they enjoy a certain autonomy, which is the very form that their existence as instances of the whole takes. This is reflected in the fact that the development of the different instances cannot be seen as part of the homogeneous development of all the instances in a common form during a unified time:

> We can argue from the specific structure of the Marxist whole that it is no longer possible to think the process of development of the different levels of the whole *in the same historical time.* Each of these different 'levels' does not have the same type of historical existence. On the contrary, we have to assign to each level a *peculiar time*, relatively autonomous and hence relatively independent, even in its dependence, of the 'times' of the other levels. . . Each of these peculiar levels is punctuated with peculiar rhythms and can only be known on condition that we have defined the *concept* of the specificity of its historical temporality and its punctuations. . . . The fact that each of these times and each of these histories is *relatively autonomous* does not make them so many domains which are *independent* of the whole: the specificity of each of these times and each of these histories – in other words, their relative autonomy and independence – is based on a certain type of *dependence* with respect to the whole.[29]

The character of the complex unity Althusser is talking about becomes now much clearer. It is one in which the superstructure, the political and the ideological, are treated as consisting of specific, distinct instances of the whole, articulated upon each other and upon the economy, but in which they are ordered by the economy in a specific relation of domination and subordination. It follows that, far from being epiphenomena of the economy, their unity with the economy is a necessary one, such that even if subordinated to the economy they are at the same time its *conditions of existence*:

> The economic dialectic is never active in *the pure state*; in History, these instances, the superstructures, etc. are never seen to step respectfully aside when their work is done, or when the time comes, as his pure phenomena, to scatter before His Majesty the Economy as he strides along the royal road to the Dialectic. From the first moment to the last, the lonely hour of the 'last instance' never comes.[30]

From the necessary unity of all the contradictory levels composing the social totality and the autonomy that each level possesses, it follows that the unity of the totality is the unity of a complex of instances at uneven stages of development relative to each other:

> If every contradiction is a contradiction in a complex whole structured in dominance, this complex whole cannot be envisaged without its contradictions, without their basically uneven relations. In other words, each contradiction, each essential articulation of the structure, and the general relation of the articulations in the structure in dominance, constitute so many conditions of existence of the complex whole itself. This proposition is of the first importance. For it means that the structure of the whole and therefore the 'difference' of the essential contradictions and their structure in dominance, is the very existence of the whole: that the 'difference' of the contradiction . . . is identical to the conditions of the existence of the complex whole.[31]

The conception of totality that emerges is one radically different from that of Hegel, and *a fortiori* from that contained in such works of mechanistic Marxism as Bukharin's *Historical Materialism*, in which the whole is simply the sum of the individual relations of cause and effect between particular events. All forms of reductionism, whether to the spiritual essence of the whole or to the economy, are ruled out by the conception of the whole as a complex unity of necessarily related but relatively autonomous instances. This does not involve a collapse into a theory of factors, since the necessary unity of the whole is the result of the structure in dominance determined by the economy:

43

Even within the reality of the conditions of existence of each contradiction, it is the manifestation of the structure in dominance that unifies the whole. *This reflection of the conditions of existence of the contradiction within itself, this reflection of the structure articulated in dominance that constitutes the unity of the complex whole within each contradiction,* this is the most profound characteristic of the Marxist dialectic, the one I have most recently tried to encapsulate in the concept of 'overdetermination'.[32]

One way of summing up the difference between the Marxist and the Hegelian dialectics would be to say that the former involves the unity of opposites and the latter the identity of opposites. To illustrate the Hegelian identity of opposites let us take the famous first triad of *Science of Logic*: Being – Nothing – Becoming. The starting point of the *Logic* is pure Being as such, because of its complete lack of any sort of determination: it is the function of the *Logic* to develop in their proper conceptual order the determinations involved in Being. However, a complete lack of determination of Being is – Nothing. Therefore, Being is its own negation, Nothing. However, Nothing negates itself, since it is precisely same lack of determination as Being. Hence, Being and Nothing are identical: their identity consists in Becoming, in the movement of the continual arising of Being and of its passing away into Nothing, which is the beginning of a process motored by the negation of the negation, in which the determinations constituting things are suppressed. And it is upon this suppression of all distinctions and determinations that the Hegelian dialectic rests: the unity of the whole consists in the identity of opposites brought about by the abolition of the determinations that constitute them.

The category of the negation of the negation clashes with the principle of non contradiction, which is the basis of both modern and ancient formal logic. This principle states that nothing can be both itself and its negation (in the modern 'formal mode', that one cannot assert both proposition P and its negation not-P) and thus recognises the distinctness of things making up the material world. The possibility of Hegel's dialectic rests on the fact that it is not ultimately a logic but a theodicy – the discovery of the unity of God and the world. The abolition of the determinations that constitute the materiality of the natural and social worlds and of the thought that its reflection can be justified only as the process whereby the world is resumed into God and all secular entities are revealed as manifestations of the Absolute Idea.

The superiority of Hegel's system over previous idealist philosophies consists in the way in which he arrives at the identity of thought and the world. Rather than being merely asserted, this identity is *developed*. Commencing from the original simple unity of Being the identity of thought and the world is developed by means of meditations into the Absolute Idea, where it collapses into another immediate unity, Nature, but a higher richer unity of Spirit, which is then again pursued through the meditations of culture and society to the highest unity of all, Absolute Knowledge or Philosophy, where the Notion recognises itself as the sum of all reality in the mind of the philosopher. The identity of thought and being is arrived at through a *process* of internal development, the dialectic. However, the structure of this dialectic is determined by its function, the resumption of material existence into the ideal. Hence its cyclical structure, hence the role of the negation of the negation as the motor of the process through the suppression of determinations. Hegel's apologists can at best isolate moments of his dialectic, for example, the articulated, complex structure of the dialectic in Book II of *The Science of Logic*, The Doctrine of Essence, while ignoring the resumption of these mediations into the spiritual unity of the Absolute Idea in Book III.[33]

The Marxist dialectic, according to Althusser, can be seen as asserting both the materiality of the world, the specificity of the entities constituting it, and, at the same time, in the case of social formations, their unity in the necessary relations of subordination and dominance characteristic of a structure in dominance. The unity of the whole does not suppress the distinctness of the determinations constituting it: rather, this distinctness is the precondition of any unity which is not the self-relation of Spirit.

There is no lack of precedent for this way of defining the difference between the two dialectics. Thus Marx writes in the 1857 Introduction the *Grundrisse*.

The conclusion we reach is not that production, distribution, exchange and consumption are identical, but that they all form the members of a totality, distinctions within a unity. Production predominates not only over itself, in the antithetical definition of production, but over the other moments as well. . . . A definite production thus determines a definite consumption, distribution and exchange as well as *definite relations between these different moments.* Admittedly, however, *in its one-sided form*, production is itself determined by the other moments. . . . Mutual interchange takes place between the different moments. This is the case with every organic whole.[34]

And Lenin writes, when describing the Marxist dialectic: 'The identity of opposites (*it would be more correct, perhaps, to say their "unity"*) is the recognition (discovery) of the contradictory, *mutually exclusive*, opposite tendencies in all phenomena.'[35]

The notion of *overdetermination* was intended by Althusser to sum up the character of the Marxist dialectic. The social totality is a complex structured unity: its complexity lies in the fact that it is a unity of distinct, relatively autonomous instances with different modes of development; its structure lies in the fact that its unity results from the hierarchy the instances possess through the determination by the economy in the final analysis. Thus the dialectic is a deterministic one in the sense that the way in which the different contradictions are articulated upon each other in the structure in dominance determines the particular direction in which the process will develop. At the same time, the unity of the whole is not a homogeneous one, it is the unity of the essentially *uneven* instances. This unevenness is not an accidental characteristic of the whole: it reflects the relative autonomy of the different instances and the different time scales according to which they develop:

Unevenness is internal to a social formation because the structuration in dominance of the complex whole, this structural invariant, *is itself the precondition for the concrete variation of the contradictions* that constitute it, and therefore for their displacements, condensations and mutations, etc., and inversely because *this variation is the existence of the invariant.*[36]

The unity of the social totality can only be grasped at any one moment by understanding it as a unity of necessarily related, necessarily uneven instances. Althusser employed the notion of *conjuncture* to express this necessary co-existence of necessarily uneven instances at a given moment – the conjuncture is the specific complex unity that a social formation reveals to analysis at any one point in time. The analysis of the conjuncture is for Althusser the foundation of Marxist politics, because the possibilities for revolution are dependent upon the particular conditions created by the uneven relations constituting a social formation. Thus Althusser takes the example of Lenin's writings in 1917;[37] these writings reveal that it was the unevenness of Russia's development – the combination of a highly advanced heavy industry with a semifeudal monarchy and agrarian system confronted with the demands of a modern interimperialist war – that rendered a socialist revolution possible in Russia before it came to the West. A similar analysis can be found in Trotsky's writings (for example, *1905*, and *The History of the Russian Revolution*), although no doubt this addition to the pedigree of the concepts of overdetermination and conjuncture would be an unwelcome one for Althusser.

Althusser attempts to clarify his admittedly difficult conception of the dialectic in *Reading Capital*, where he introduces the notion of *structural causality*. For the account of overdetermination in *For Marx* leaves us with a problem. In formal terms, the structure of the social whole is fairly clearly defined. The assignment by the economy of á particular instance to the dominant role unifies the whole. This unity is said to consist in the presence of the structure in dominance in each of its conditions of existence, i.e. in each of the contradictions constituting the whole. The epistemological sense of the redrawing of the relation between whole and parts still needs to be spelled out.

This is the last major question Althusser sets himself in *Reading Capital*:

> *By means of what concepts, or what set of concepts, is it possible to think the determination of the elements of a structure, and the structural relations between these elements, and all the effects of these relations, by the effectivity of that structure? And a fortiori, by means*

of what concept or what set of concepts is it possible to think the determination of a subordinate structure; in other words, how is it possible to define the concept of a structural causality?[38]

The problem is an especially acute one in the case of *Capital* because of the theory of fetishism it contains. The theory of fetishism explains how the exploitation of the proletariat – the extraction of surplus value in the productive process – which is the foundation of the capitalist mode of production, is systematically concealed. The key passage for this analysis is, of course, the section of Chapter 1 of *Capital*, Volume I, entitled 'The Fetishism of Commodities'. Rather than appearing as they are – the products of social labour – commodities appear as things whose functioning is dependent, not upon the social relations of production, but on their mutual interrelations in the market. This serves to mask the exploitation upon which the generalised exchange of commodities depends.[39] Fetishism also reveals itself in the division of surplus value into profit, rent and interest, which gives rise to the 'Trinity Formula' of vulgar political economy. According to this formula, there are three sources of value, land, labour and capital, from which derive the three forms of income, rent, wages (profit is subsumed under this head as the 'wages of management') and interest. Thus, in one movement, the real source of value – labour – is masked, and the exploitation of the worker is justified as resulting from the need for both labour and means of production in the productive process.[40] It is in terms of the theory of fetishism that the celebrated distinction arises, between the essence of the capitalist mode of production and the phenomenal form in which it appears to the agents of production.

However, the form in which the capitalist mode of production is manifested cannot be reduced to an opposition between the real underlying essence and the illusory appearances. Rather, it is a process in which is the capitalist mode of production is both presented and concealed in one movement; the result is not pure illusion – it is a *necessary* feature of that mode of production.[41] The fetished and estranged appearance that the mode of production takes on results from mechanisms that are the necessary conditions for the functioning of the system as such. For, while the system rests upon the extraction of surplus value from the worker in the immediate production process, the manner in which the social character of the labour that produces commodities is established under capitalism is not through any sort of direct regulation but rather through the generalised exchange of commodities on the market. Therefore the reproduction of the capitalist mode of production is dependent upon the mechanisms of the market:

> In this entirely specific form of value [that of exchange value], labour prevails on the one hand as social labour; on the other hand, the distribution of this social labour and the mutual supplementing and interchanging of its products, the subordination under, and introduction into, the social mechanism, are left to the accidental and mutually nullifying motives of individual capitalists. Since these latter confront one another only as commodity-owners and everyone seeks to sell his commodity as dearly as possible (apparently even guided in the regulation of production itself solely by his free will), the inner law enforces itself only through their competition, their mutual pressure upon each other, whereby the deviations are mutually cancelled. Only as an inner law, *vis-à-vis* the individual agents, as a blind law of Nature, does the law of value exert its influence here and maintain the social equilibrium of production amidst its accidental fluctuations.[42]

Thus fetishism is not simply an illusory appearance. It is the *mode of existence* of capitalist production. The mystified character of the system results not from some accidental feature of it, or from the skill of the capitalists in fooling workers, but from its very heart, from the nature of the commodity, that is, from the very form that the products of labour must take under the capitalist mode of production. A commodity is a use value produced by human labour which cannot be directly consumed because of the social division of labour, but whose consumption is dependent on its exchange in the market. The exchange of commodities is regulated by their values, that is, by the amount of labour-time socially necessary for their production. However, the value of a commodity, although it is created in the direct production process by the labour of the workers, is only established for society in the form of its exchange value and price in the market. The law of value only has application through the obscuring relationships of the market. This is also so in the case of the Trinity

Formula. The division of surplus value into profit, interest and rent is a necessary precondition for the reproduction of the capitalist mode of production: it is only thereby that the capitalist secures the prerequisites for continued production – land and capital – and the surplus to reinvest in extended production. But:

> It is clear that, as soon as surplus value (is split up) into different, *separate* parts, related to various production elements – such as nature, products, labour – which only differ *physically*, that is, as soon as in general surplus value acquires *special* forms, separate from one another and regulated by different laws, the common unit – surplus value – and consequently the nature of the common unit, becomes more and more unrecognisable and does not manifest itself in the *appearance* but has to be discovered as a hidden mystery.[43]

The character of the capitalist mode of production, as analysed by Marx in *Capital* and *Theories of Surplus Value*, is that of a structure which dissimulates itself in presenting itself.[44] The problem, then, for Althusser is to construct a concept of causality which can express the relation between a structure which is a 'hidden mystery', and its effects, which serve to conceal it in manifesting it. His solution is to conceive the causality of the structure in dominance on the contradictions constituting the social totality as one that is nothing beyond the interrelation of those contradictions. The causality of the whole consists in the relations subsisting between its effects:

> The structure is not an essence *outside* the economic phenomena which comes and alters their aspect, forms and relations which is effective upon them as an absent cause, *absent because it is outside them. The absence of the cause in the structure's 'metonymic causality' on its effects is not the fault of the exteriority of the structure with respect to the economic phenomena; on the contrary, it is the very form of the interiority of the structure, in its effects.* This implies therefore that the effects are not outside the structure, are not a pre-existing object, element or space in which the structure arrives to *imprint its mark*: on the contrary, it implies that the structure is immanent in its effects, a cause immanent in its effects in the Spinozist sense of the term, that *the whole existence of the structure consists of its effects*, in short that the structure, which is merely a specific combination of its peculiar elements, is nothing outside its effects.[45]

50

Althusser does not develop the concept of structural causality in *Reading Capital*, preferring instead to use it as a way of detailing his conception of the sciences as a process taking place entirely in thought. This provides a cue for how we should treat the concept of structural causality, its role reflecting Althusser's epistemological preoccupations. He wants to attack the classical distinction between phenomenon and essence, where phenomenon is a subjective veil of illusion that can be separated from, peeled off, reality. Instead, as we have seen in Marx's treatment of fetishism, the appearances that the capitalist relations of productions take up, form its necessary mode of existence. But more importantly, for Althusser, the essence/phenomenon distinction is connected with the empiricist theory of reading, according to which the essence is immediately present in the appearances. For, if the appearances are subjective illusion then an informed gaze can pierce them, grasping the hidden essence. Thought's ability to comprehend the real becomes dependent on the structure of the real, the way in which it separates off into essence and phenomenon.

The other side of the coin to the rejection of the veil of illusion treatment of the appearances, is the abandonment of the idea of essence as an immediately accessible entity lurking just beneath the phenomenon awaiting our searching gaze. This notion of essence underlies both what Althusser calls linear causality, the classical empiricist idea of the relation of cause and effect as a pattern linking observed events, and expressive causality, the idealist detection of the meaning of the whole in every one of its parts. Instead the essence has become a structure dispersed among its elements, a cause that 'is nothing outside its effects', that can only be grasped by constructing the scientific concepts that express the relations between its elements.

This approach is less daunting than it might seem. It is implied in the notion of overdetermination. Overdetermination, we should recall, is the idea of a structure whose complexity, the mutual distinctness and interdependence of its elements, is expressed through the way in which the economy displaces the dominant role within the structure to a particular instance, organising the other instances in terms of this structure in dominance. Clearly, then, given these displacements, the causality governing each element is not one that can be attributed to any discrete cause, but rather to the structure of the whole as determined by the economy in the last instance. What Althusser is trying to hammer home to us is the shift from treating a cause as a thing, a substance, a distinct, separately identifiable entity to treating it as a relation, from something that can be immediately or ultimately pointed to, grasped hold of, to treating it as the displacements effected by the structure of a whole upon its elements. What the structure is is quite straightforward: it is the mechanism of overdetermination and determination in the last instance. Althusser is here giving an epistemological twist to the concepts of the dialectic he has already developed, spelling out the relation between his critique of empiricism and the theory of overdetermination. Both his own theory of overdetermination and Marx's theory of fetishism lead Althusser to the conclusion that the appearances are not something dispensable, mere subjective illusion, but the necessary form reality takes. He has now reversed the point, to argue that reality is not something underlying the appearances, but is the structured relation of these appearances.

On the face of it this would seem to be a form of atomism that reduces the whole to the sum of its parts. Yet it is not so, since causal and epistemological priority is given to the structured whole. What Althusser wants to attack is the sort of empiricism that makes the whole something present in, yet separable from, its parts. For him whole and parts are inseparable and the whole is present in the relation of its effects. Thus the economy is determinant in the last instance not because the other instances are its epiphenonema but because it determines which instance is dominant. Its role can only be grasped by the relations constituting the structure of the whole, only through the mode in which the elements of the whole are articulated upon each other.

Structural causality thus in a sense sums up Althusser's theory of the dialectic and his theory of reading. Together they assign a central role to ideology, to the structures whose specific role is to mystify the workings of social formations, and to the science of historical materialism which can decode the complexities of the social whole. Let us go on, then, to consider the sciences and ideology.

The Autonomy of Theory

Althusser's system, as expounded in *For Marx* and *Reading Capital* involves a theory of practices. A social formation involves a number of distinct practices united in a complex whole. Although these practices are distinct, they can be subsumed under the same general definition:

> By *practice* in general I shall mean any process of *transformation* of a determinate given raw material into a determinate *product*, a transformation effected by a determinate human labour, using determinate means ('of production'). In any practice thus conceived, the *determinant* moment (or element) is neither the raw material nor the product, but the practice in the narrow sense: the moment of the *labour of transformation* itself, which sets to work, in a specific structure, men, means and a technical method of utilising the means. This general definition of practice covers the possibility of particularity: there are different practices which are really distinct even though they belong organically to the same complex totality. Thus 'social practice', the complex unity of the practices existing in a determinate society, contains a large number of distinct practices.[46]

Out of this 'large number' of practices composing the social totality, we only hear of three apart from production itself: political, ideological and theoretical practice. Significantly, political practice is only discussed in relation to ideology,[47] which I shall discuss below. But first let us look at the theory of the sciences contained in *For Marx* and *Reading Capital*.

We must first step back to see the role Althusser's theory of the sciences has for his work as a whole, and how it relates to the problems of Marxist philosophy discussed in the first chapter. It is of significance at two related levels. In the first place, there is what might be called the purely epistemological dimension. That is to say, there is the task of characterising the sciences as practices, whose function it is to produce objective knowledges, the task of both articulating the internal structures of the sciences and specifying their relation to their real objects, the reality of which they are knowledges. We should note here that for Althusser, as is the case with many contemporary philosophers of science, the significance of the sciences lies less in the

53

particular results arrived at, than in *the way in which* they are arrived at. Rather than from propositions like the Newtonian laws of motion, scientificity derives from what Lakatos called *heuristic*, the theoretical structures that made their discovery possible. We could call this the *problem of scientificity*, the problem of the methods whereby we determine whether or not a theoretical formation is scientific and analyse the processes whereby it develops.

Secondly, the problem of scientificity is not an abstract one for Althusser: it relates to the *scientificity of Marxism*. This raises a question specific to Marxism: *the problem of the unity of theory and practice*. Although this is above all a political problem, it is also a theoretical one which has proved to be of the first importance for Marxist philosophy. What is the relation between the science of history and the struggles of the working class? How is the unity of Marxism and the proletariat in the revolutionary struggle to be achieved and maintained? I have shown that these two problems, those of scientificity and of the unity of theory and practice, greatly exercised Lukacs, Gramsci and Korsch. I have argued that their positions were undermined by conflating the two problems. The problems are also present in Althusser's work. If the first, that of scientificity, is very much to the fore in *For Marx* and *Reading Capital*, the second is also present, if only as part of the underplot, and comes more to light in Althusser's recent writings.

The character of Althusser's solution has been invariant throughout his work. (Or, better: his reformulation of the *problem* has remained invariant, although in his later writings Althusser has come to recognise that to reformulate a problem is not necessarily to solve it.) The fundamental resting point of his position has been the thesis that *theory is autonomous*. Theoretical practice is a distinct and autonomous practice which is not reducible to the other instances of the social formation. The alternative would be to treat the sciences as ideologies, as theories which reflect, and are subordinated to, the situation and interests of particular classes. This path was the one taken by Lukacs and Gramsci. The result was that it became impossible to establish the objectivity of the sciences. The validity of the sciences became dependent, in Lukacs's case, on their character as the con-

54

sciousness of a given class-subject. In Gramsci it depended, immediately, on their role in articulating the aspirations of a particular class to hegemony over society and, ultimately, on an anticipated unity of mankind in which objectivity is the unanimity of a humanity free at last from class conflict.

The anomaly in this approach, particularly in Lukacs's case, is the position of the natural sciences. If they are ideologies, as he implies when he criticises their passive, abstract, one-sided nature, then we must agree with Korsch that:

> The real contradiction between Marx's scientific socialism and all bourgeois philosophy *and sciences* consists entirely in the fact that scientific socialism is the theoretical expression of a revolutionary process, which will end with the total abolition of all those bourgeois philosophies and sciences, together with the abolition of the material relations which find their ideological expression in them.[48]

In this case, it seems difficult to see how we can avoid the position, banal as it is absurd, that it will be necessary to construct a proletarian physics and chemistry to replace the bourgeois natural sciences. This position was taken seriously albeit briefly at the height of Zhdanov's reign over Russian culture in the 1940s. However, there seems no good reason why we should take it seriously until someone outlines in detail how the abolition of capitalism will affect the content of, say, special and general relativity theory.

To sum up, the Hegelian reduction of the sciences to first another element of the superstructure like politics and ideology leads to a slide into subjectivism. If, on the other hand, the sciences are not ideologies, it is incumbent upon us to construct a theory of the sciences as deriving their objective status from an, at least relative, autonomy from the other practices that constitute the social formation.[49]

If we assert that the sciences, and the theoretical ideologies that constitute their prehistory, which together make up the instance Althusser calls theoretical practice, are (relatively) autonomous, then it follows that the process whereby objective knowledges of the real are produced takes place entirely *in thought*. We have already encountered this thesis in the form of the distinction that Althusser

55

makes between the real object of a science and its thought-object. Althusser is concerned to emphasise that he is not, however, counterposing pure thought and the world:

> Far from being an essence opposed to the material world, the faculty of a 'pure' transcendental subject or 'absolute consciousness', i.e. the myth that idealism produces as a myth in which to recognise and establish itself, 'thought' is a peculiar real system, established on and articulated to the real world of a given historical society which maintains determinate relations with nature, a *specific* system, defined by its conditions of existence and practice, i.e. by a *peculiar structure*, a determinate type of 'combination' (*Verbindung*) between its peculiar raw material (the object of theoretical practice), its peculiar means of production and its relations with the other structures of society.[50]

As we have seen, for Althusser, to characterise knowledge as a practice implies more than an assertion of its material and social nature: it involves a particular analysis of how knowledge is produced in accordance with the general definition of practice in *For Marx*. Taking up Marx's famous description of 'the scientifically correct method' of political economy as 'rising from the abstract to the concrete',[51] he employs the general theory of practice to elaborate this definition. To understand the process of theoretical practice involves distinguishing between three bodies of concepts at work in the process, called Generalities I, II and III. Generality I forms the starting point, the raw material of theoretical practice, that is to say, the body of *concepts* (not, to repeat, things in the world), either scientific or ideological, upon which the process will set to work in order to transform them. Generality II is the corpus of concepts whose more or less contradictory unity constitutes the 'theory' of the science in question by defining the field in which the problems of the science must necessarily be posed – in other words, the science's problematic. Generality III is the 'concrete-in-thought', the knowledge that is produced by the work of Generality II on Generality I, of the concepts defined by the science's problematic on the pre-existing theories that constitute the pre-history of this stage in the science's development.

A correct understanding of theoretical practice can only be reached, Althusser argues, if two theses are accepted. Firstly, there is never any identity of essence between Generalities I and III, the process's raw material and end product respectively, but always a real transformation. The process of knowledge does not involve the rendering explicit of what was always implicit, a procession of stages *within the Absolute*, but the production of new knowledges, and sometimes the revolutionary overthrow of a problematic. We find examples of the latter when a science emerges from its ideological prehistory by means of an epistemological break, or when the problematic of a science is recast, as Kepler recast the problematic of astronomy.[52] Secondly, the work whereby Generality I becomes Generality III, whereby the 'abstract' becomes 'concrete', involves only the process of theoretical practice, that is to say, it takes place 'within thought'. This involves a break, not only with the historicist reduction of science to the superstructure, but also with all forms of empiricism, which makes the scientificity of a theory dependent upon the immediate relation held to exist between that theory and the real, whether the relation takes the form of verification, induction, falsification or any other device characteristic of the bourgeois philosophy of science. We can easily see that such theories are a special case of the epistemology criticised in the first section of this chapter for its reliance upon a pre-established harmony, an underlying complicity, between subject and object, thought and the real.[53]

A problem immediately arises for Althusser. He has rejected both the epistemology most characteristic of bourgeois philosophy and that associated with the most intellectually rich and sophisticated strands in the Marxist tradition. How, then, is the scientificity of a theory to be established? This is especially important since he has rested so much upon the scientificity of Marxism and upon the sharp break between historical materialism and its ideological prehistory which he asserts took place in 1845. How, then, are we to distinguish between a science and an ideology, since both are to be found in the process of knowledge? Althusser recognises the problem:

> *By what mechanism does the process of knowledge, which takes place entirely in thought, produce the cognitive appropriation of its real object, which exists outside thought in the real world? Or again, by what mechanism does the production of the object of knowledge produce the cognitive appropriation of the real object, which exists outside thought in the real world?*[54]

57

In the same movement as he poses the question, Althusser rules out certain answers. These answers all take the form of attempting to find *guarantees* external to a theory for the scientificity of that theory. All must be ruled out because all rest upon the problematic we have encountered before, which defines knowledge as a direct relation between real and thought objects, resting it upon a complicity between subject and object, perhaps in their identity. This search for guarantees is characteristic, he asserts, of all bourgeois philosophy: even sceptics like Hume defined knowledge in terms of the relation between subject and object, although they asserted that such a relation is unattainable. Similarly, we can see that it is true of much of Marxist philosophy. Thus Engels seeks to guarantee the validity of the dialectic by founding it upon certain general laws which govern the whole of reality, and govern thought as its reflection.

Any attempt to justify a science by giving it a foundation external to it comes up against the same objection. It must be rejected because it is ideological. Rather than recognising that the scientific character of a theory rests on its openness to development, such an approach tries to rest it on a predetermined relation between that theory and its real object. As we shall see, for Althusser ideology always involves a guarantee through a pre-established harmony between subject and object.[55]

> The mere substitution of the question of the *mechanism* of cognitive appropriation of the real object of knowledge by means of the object of knowledge, for the ideological question of *guarantees* of the possibility of knowledge, contains in it that mutation which rescues us from the closed space of ideology and opens to us the open space of the philosophical theory we are seeking.[56]

For this, according to Althusser, is the role of Marxist philosophy: rather than trying vainly to erect itself into the guarantor of the sciences, thereby transforming itself into the spokesman of ideology, Marxist philosophy must be the 'theory of theoretical practice' – must analyse the mechanisms responsible for 'the "*knowledge–effect*" which is the peculiarity of those special products which are knowledges'.[57] Marxist philosophy, the theory of theoretical practice, concerns itself with the question of the mechanisms that result in the emergence of theoretical formations that are scientific, i.e. that achieve a genuine cognitive appropriation of the real rather than a mystical reflection of conditions anterior to theory as do the ideologies that masquerade as science. Althusser leaves the matter here, but not before describing the autonomy of theoretical practice in such a way as to make any return to an ideological problematic of guarantees impossible:

> *Theoretical practice* is . . . its own criterion and contains in itself definite protocols with which to *validate* the quality of its product, i.e. the criteria of the scientificity of the products of theoretical practice. This is exactly what happens in the real practice of the sciences: once they are truly constituted and developed they have no need for verification from *external* practices to declare the knowledges they produce to be 'true', i.e. to be *knowledges*. At least for the most developed of them and in the areas of knowledges they have sufficiently mastered, they themselves provide the criterion of validity of the knowledges – this criterion coinciding perfectly with the strict forms of the exercise of the scientific practices considered.[58]

This passage is of the first importance not simply because it is the most thoroughgoing assertion of the autonomy of theory that Althusser has made, but because it involves a solution to the problem of scientificity. The solution is – that there is no solution. *There is no general criterion of scientificity.* The 'radical inwardness' of theoretical practice rules out the possibility of such a general criterion since it would be the product, not of the particular sciences themselves, but of a practice external to them. To assert the necessity of such a criterion would be to remain within the problematic of guarantees.

Yet, how can we reconcile this thesis with Althusser's conception of Marxist philosophy as the theory of theoretical practice? For the only difference between the analysis of the knowledge-effect provided by the theory of theoretical practice and the general criterion of scientificity that Althusser argues we must reject as ideological is that in the case of the former we are offered the promise, if not the reality, of a *causal* analysis of the foundations of science. But in essence the theory of theoretical practice is a theory of the difference between science and ideology. Since it is responsible for *establishing* scientificity as such the theory must involve a general criterion of scientificity. It would seem that Althusser has been unable to transcent the problematic of bourgeois epistemology. This contradiction, which clearly exists in the texts published in *Reading Capital*, did not arise by chance. We shall examine its necessary place within Althusser's system, and its destiny in his work, in the next chapter.

The second problem, that of the unity of theory and practice, is one to which there is little explicit reference in *For Marx* and *Reading Capital*. Such as there is, is deeply unsatisfactory. For Althusser informs us that his theory of practices, and his characterisation of theory as theoretical *practice* abolishes the problem. Within theoretical practice itself there exists the unity of theory and practice in the work performed by Generality II on Generality I in transforming it into Generality III. Since theory is itself a practice, the whole problem of the unity of theory and practice is revealed as a pseudo-problem. Regis Debray, who studied under Althusser, sums this approach up succinctly:

> Theory draws its effectiveness from its rigorousness, and its rigorousness is effective because it separates 'development in reality' from 'development in thought', the 'operation of society' from the 'operation of knowledge'. In other words, all we had to do to become good theoreticians was to be lazy bastards.[59]

This is all the comment this 'solution' merits. However, we will have to return to it in the next chapter for the light it throws on the character of Althusser's system.

The Objectivity of Appearance

We have already encountered Marx's theory of fetishism, which treats the estranged appearance of the capitalist mode of production not as pure illusion or deception, but as the necessary form it takes on in order to function. The theory of fetishism is the kernel of the theory of ideology which we owe to Marx. It may be summed up in a phrase of Hegel's – 'the Objectivity of Appearance'.[60] Lenin expresses the point very well:

60

> Hegel is for the 'objective validity' . . . of Semblance, of that which is immediately given. . . . The more petty philosophers dispute whether essence *or* that which is immediately given should be taken as basis. . . . Instead of *or*, Hegel puts *and*, explaining the concrete content of this 'and'.[61]

The same could be said of Marx, with the proviso that he does not reabsorb both 'essence' and 'appearance' into the Absolute Idea, as Hegel does in the second volume of the *Logic*. We have also seen the philosophical importance which Althusser attaches to the notion of ideology in his account of Marx's theoretical development. We must now turn to the general theory which this account presupposes.

The best way into Althusser's theory of ideology is through a couple of the most common misunderstandings about the nature of ideology. We have already encountered the treatment of ideology as mere deception or illusion. One of the major themes of Althusser's work, in common with that of Lukacs and Korsch, is to emphasise the objective role that ideology plays in social formations:

> An ideology is a system (with its own logic and rigour) of representations (images, myths, ideas or concepts, depending on the case) endowed with a historical existence and role within a given society.[62]

Secondly (and this an error common even in Marxist circles), the ideological character of a system of representations derives not from any political presuppositions or implications it may possess but from its mystified and mystifying structure:

> In ideology men do indeed express, not the relation between them and their conditions of existence, but *the way* they live the relation between them and their real conditions of existence. In ideology the real relation is inevitably invested in the imaginary relation, a relation that *expresses a will* (conservative, conformist, reformist or revolutionary), a hope or a nostalgia, rather than describing a reality.[63]

These are in fact the essentials of Althusser's analysis of ideology in *For Marx* and *Reading Capital*. Ideology is the mystified form in which men experience their relation to the world. Althusser does not add the qualification which one might have expected: 'except in classless societies'. On the contrary:

Ideology (as a system of mass representations) is indispensable in any society if men are to be formed, transformed and equipped to respond to the demands of their conditions of existence.[64]

We learn, therefore, that ideology has a role to play even in communist society, since even under communism it will be necessary that men be adapted to fulfill adequately the demands society has to make on them. The difference presumably would be that under communism the demands would be those of a non-exploitative society, rather than, as previously, those of a class society. We shall return to this claim.

For the moment, it is worth noting the skeletal character of Althusser's account of ideology. Beyond the remarks I have already quoted about the closed nature of ideology,[65] we are given no real idea of where the mystifying character of ideology lies. Nor are we given any account of the mechanisms whereby ideology is imposed on the masses. We do learn that there are two kinds of ideologies – theoretical and practical ideologies. The latter immediately inhabit men's everyday practice, the former are part of the process of theoretical practice. Of the distinction between science and ideology we learn only that 'ideology, as a system of representations, is distinguished from science in that in it the practico-social function is more important than the theoretical function'.[66] Of the mechanisms whereby, through an epistemological break, a science emerges from an ideology, we are told nothing. There is a major difficulty to be dealt with here: we cannot invoke the machinery of Generalities I, II and III, for the transformation of an ideological Generality I into a scientific Generality III involves the work of a scientific problematic invested in Generality II and Marx's epistemological break took precisely the form of a change of problematics, rather than a production of knowledges. This latter task had to wait upon the work of the new problematic on classical political economy, resulting in *Capital*. So how was the new, scientific problematic produced? We shall return to this problem also in the next chapter.

The gaps to which I have referred are partially filled in a more recent text of Althusser's *Ideology and Ideological State Apparatuses*, which both develops and adds to the theses advanced in *For Marx*. He starts by criticising the purely metaphorical and descriptive character of the base/superstructure opposition, that is a standard feature of orthodox treatments of the role of ideology and the state. He argues that it is by locating the role of the superstructure in securing the reproduction of the mode of production that we can arrive at a scientific theory of the superstructure. This insight is not systematically developed, but as it stands it does seem to have some force: the role of ideology and the state is strictly determined by their contribution, not so much directly to the immediate production process, as to securing the conditions necessary for the continued reproduction of the social formation. Such preconditions would include for example a docile labour force, the ability to employ sufficient force to crush any potential threat to the system (which may not be possible through direct use of the state but may rather involve the mobilisation of the ideological resources of the ruling class, e.g. the exploitation by big capitalists of bourgeois and petit bourgeois ideology in order to use fascist mass parties to smash the workers' movement, the use of the mass media to stultify independent and critical thought, and so on).

Althusser puts forward two theses on ideology, which he proceeds to develop:

> THESIS I: Ideology represents the imaginary relationships of individuals to their real conditions of existence.[67]
> THESIS II: Ideology has a material existence.[68]

We have already encountered the first thesis, and the second was contained in the notion of the objective historical role played by ideology. However, the way in which it is developed is novel. I shall deal with the latter thesis first, the former is closely related to the conclusion of this chapter.

> Where only a single subject (such and such an individual) is concerned, the existence of the ideas of his [ideological – AC] belief is material in that *his ideas are his material actions inserted into material practices governed by material rituals which are themselves defined by the material ideological apparatus from which derives the ideas of that subject.*[69]

Despite the repetition of the word 'material' like an incantation, we can see that the materiality of a set of ideological beliefs derives from the

63

fact that they are, firstly, embodied in particular social practices, and, secondly, the products of what Althusser calls an *Ideological State Apparatus* (ISA). He argues, following Gramsci, that we must see the political power of a ruling class as consisting in, not simply their monopoly of the repressive apparatus of the state, the army, police and so on, but also their ideological hegemony over society, embodied in the institutionalisation of their ideology in various apparatuses appertaining, not so much to the state in the strict sense, but rather to what in bourgeois terms are called the private activities of citizens, what Gramsci calls civil society.

Althusser accordingly distinguishes between two types of State Apparatus, the Repressive State Apparatus, and the Ideological State Apparatuses. Examples of the latter are the churches, schools, universities, trade unions, political parties. He sums up the distinctions between the two types of State Apparatus very lucidly:

1. All the State Apparatuses function both by repression and by ideology, with the difference that the (Repressive) State Apparatus functions incisively and predominantly by repression, whereas the Ideological State Apparatuses function massively and predominantly by ideology.

2. Whereas the (Repressive) State Apparatus constitutes an organized whole whose different parts are centralized beneath a commanding unity, that of the politics of class struggle applied by the political representatives of the ruling classes in possession of state power, the Ideological State Apparatuses are multiple, distinct, 'relatively autonomous' and capable of providing an objective field to contradictions which express, in forms which may be limited or extreme, the effects of the clashes between the capitalist class struggle and the proletarian class struggle, as well as their subordinate forms.

3. Whereas the unity of the (Repressive) State Apparatus is secured by its unified and centralised organization under the leadership of the representatives of the classes in power executing the politics of the class struggle of the classes in power, the unity of the different Ideological State Apparatuses is secured, usually in contradictory forms, by the ruling ideology, the ideology of the ruling class.[70]

Thus Althusser's account of the materiality of ideology sends us

64

back once again to examine the nature of ideology as such, i.e. the manner in which it produces an account of the world which is adequate for those who live in ideology to perform the roles demanded of them by society and yet mystifies the relation between them and their conditions of existence. We can start from the function it fulfills: that of adapting individuals so as to enable them to respond to the needs of society. It succeeds in fulfilling this function, according to Althusser, by means of the operation of the category of the subject. For, '*all ideology hails or interpellates concrete individuals as concrete subjects*, by the functioning of the category of the subject.'[71]

The notion that the category of the subject is constitutive of all ideology is among the most obscure features of Althusser's position. Essentially what he seems to be saying is this. The category of the subject can fulfill the function of ideology, of adapting individuals to the demands society makes on them, because it presupposes the notion of an underlying and predetermined complicity between subject and object. The notion of a subject cannot be separated from that of its object, and from the relation held to subsist between them. In a sense, subject and object are *made for* each other. To conceive of a subject is to conceive of whatever it is the subject *of*. To conceive of an object is to conceive of whatever it is an object *for*. The world, his object, is ultimately meaningful for the human subject for one of two reasons. Either, the subject has imposed a meaning on the world, that is, he has (in a sense) created his object, as, for example, philosophers of the phenomenological school have argued. Alternatively, the subject is a creation of his object, in which case the object is thereby transformed into a subject. This is true most obviously in the case of all forms of deism and theism, but also in the case of many versions of materialism, where nature becomes the omnipotent Subject in the place of God. We can say, therefore, that the category of the subject is a theological one, since it involves either the notion of God (or a God-like Nature) or the transformation of man into a God, by making him creator of the world.

The category of the subject is therefore uniquely fitted to the purpose of ideology since the complicity of subject and object that underlies it gives the world a meaning *for the individual* that suppresses

65

the mechanisms of exploitation and oppression at the heart of society and the meaningless chaos at its surface. Both are abolished in a system of ideal relationships which picks out each individual, giving him a unique value by virtue of the relation that exists between him and the world under their aspect of subject and object respectively. We can assume that ideology will take the form of transforming the world into a subject that has created the individual rather than (outside philosophy and various pathological mental states) endowing the individual with the attributes of a God:

> The structure of all ideology, interpellating individuals as subjects in the name of a Unique and Absolute Subject is *speculary*, i.e. a mirror-structure, and *doubly* speculary: this mirror duplication is constitutive of ideology and ensures its functioning. Which means that all ideology is *centred*, that the Absolute Subject occupies the unique place of the Centre, and interpellates around it the infinity of individuals into subjects in a double mirror-connection such that it *subjects* the subjects to the Subject, while giving them in the Subject, in which each subject can contemplate its own image (present and future) the *guarantee* that this really concerns them and Him, and that since everything takes place in the Family (the Holy Family: the Family is in essence Holy), 'God will *recognise* his own in it', i.e. those who have recognised God, and have recognised themselves in Him, will be saved.[72]

The subordination of the individual to the demands of society results from the guarantee that the structure of the subject/object relation offers. By placing the individual in a structure which enables him to recognise himself in the world, to see it as a world in a sense created for him, in which there is a place for him, an assurance is offered that if he conforms with what is required of him by society, all will be well for him.

The Process without a Subject

In several recent texts Althusser has deployed this critique of the category of the subject to express both the essence of his position and the relation that exists between the Marxist and Hegelian dialectics in the thesis that Marxism rests on the notion of history as *a process without a subject*:

66

To be dialectical materialist, Marxist philosophy must break with the idealist category of the 'Subject' as Origin, Essence and Cause, *responsible* in its *interiority* for all the determinations of the external 'Object', whose internal 'Subject' it is called.[73]

Althusser introduces this concept in discussing Marx's relation to Hegel. That is to say, he returns to the problem that confronted him in the essays that were to become *For Marx*, the question of the specificity of the Marxist dialectic, of the differences between it and the Hegelian system. However, he begins this time by stressing the positive aspects of Hegel's philosophy:

There is no trace (in Feuerbach) of the theory of history we owe to Hegel as *a dialectical process of production of forms (figures)*.

Of course . . . what immediately disfigures the Hegelian conception of History, as a dialectical process is its *teleological* conception of the dialectic, inscribed in the structures of the dialectic at an extremely precise point: the *Aufhebung* (transcendence-preserving the transcended-as-the-internalised-transcended), directly expressed in the Hegelian category of the *negation of the negation* (or negativity).[74]

We have already encountered the category of the negation of the negation as the key to an understanding of the difference between the Marxist and the Hegelian dialectics. The function this category plays in abolishing the determinations making up the material world and resuming them in the Absolute Idea is effected by transforming them into transcended-but-preserved (the famous *Aufhebung*) stages in the process of reaching a predetermined goal. The course the process will take is determined from and in its beginnings. Thus Hegel writes of the point at which the science of logic must begin:

What is essential for the Science is not so much that a pure immediate is the beginning, but that itself in its totality forms a cycle returning upon itself, wherein the first is also last and the last first.[75]

Thus both Hegel's *Phenomenology* and his *Logic* describe circles in which the beginning is an immediate unity and the process consists in the development of the mediations implicit in that unity until they are resumed into a form of the Absolute, and collapse into an immediate unity, but a higher unity, pregnant with richer mediations, a stage in the progress of the Absolute towards self-realisation. For this of course is the goal of the process: the identity of thought and being in the Absolute.

An understanding of the teleological and hence idealist character of the master categories of Hegel's dialectic creates a paradoxical situation for those who believe that this dialectic can be simply adapted for other, materialist, purposes:

> To criticise the Hegelian philosophy of History because it is *teleological*, because from its origin it is in pursuit of a goal (the realisation of the Absolute Knowledge), hence to reject the teleology in the philosophy of History, but to return to the Hegelian dialectic as such at the same time, is to fall into a strange contradiction. For the Hegelian dialectic, too, is teleological in its *structures*, since the key structures of the Hegelian dialectic is the *negation of the negation*, *which is the teleology itself*, within the dialectic.[76]

What then did the Marxist dialectic derive from Hegel?

> Once one is prepared to consider just for a moment that the whole Hegelian teleology is contained in the expressions I have just stated, in the categories of alienation, or in what constitutes the master structure of the category of the dialectic (the negation of the negation) and once one accepts, if that is possible, to *abstract* from what represents the teleology in these expressions, then there remains the formulation: *history is a process without a subject*. I think I can affirm: this category of *a process without a subject*, which must of course be torn from the grip of the Hegelian teleology, undoubtedly represents the greatest theoretical debt linking Marx to Hegel.[77]

Once freed from the teleology of the negation of the negation, which suppresses the specificity of the instances of the social totality into the spirituality of a simple whole, the notion of the process without a subject, of history motored by the peculiar articulations of the contradictions internal to it, can serve as foundation of the materialist dialectic. Herein lay Marx's novelty.

For even the Hegelian dialectic possesses a subject, albeit 'a very strange subject . . . this subject is the very *teleology* of the *process*,

68

it is the *Idea*, in the process of self-alienation which constitutes it as the Idea'.[78] The Absolute Idea is never embodied in any entity, it is something that exists only in the process of its self-realisation, *in the very dialectic itself*. The culmination of the dialectic lies in the recognition of reality as its creation by the subject of the process, the Absolute Idea. But the Absolute's being does not consist in any identifiable individuality; it consists in the very structure of the process, the sucession of circles whose point of arrival and departure is the same – the identity of thought and being in the Absolute. This is how Hegel set the stage for Marx. All that was required to develop a dialectic that would open up history to scientific knowledge was to transform the structure of the dialectic, to remove its peculiar subject, the self-reflection of the process, by abolishing the category whose function it was to realise that subject in the process, the negation of the negation. This was not something that occurred in the *Manuscripts* of 1844: there Marx simply removed the speculative notion of the Absolute Idea from its place as subject of history and replaced it with that of the human essence. History still had a subject: hence the teleological structure of the dialectic in the *Manuscripts*, the drama of man's alienation under capitalism and reconciliation with himself under communism in accordance with a predetermined necessity immanent in history. The decisive point came when Marx began, in 1845, to develop concepts like forces and relations of production capable of grasping history as a process without a subject.

What does the notion of process without a subject imply? In the first place, that history develops in accordance with the particular overdetermined configuration that the contradictions constituting it at any one time take. All ideas of history developing in accordance with an immanent necessity towards a predetermined goal must be rejected. History is a process whose end is not fixed in its origins, although the particular overdetermined relation of its contradictions will weight its development in a particular direction. Secondly, it involved a rejection of any notion of human nature in general, at least of any such notion which involved a claim to an explanatory role in the science of history. This is the burden of Althusser's celebrated 'theoretical anti-humanism': the denial that the human essence is the subject of history and that it determines its direction according to a predestined drama of alienation and reconciliation.

Finally, it implies that the role that human individuals play in history as *individuals* is that of the embodiments of the process, not as its subjects. Taking up various passages in *Capital*,[79] Althusser argues that individuals must be seen as the agents of the mode of production, in the role of capitalists, workers, etc. according to the positions to which they are assigned through the mechanisms reproducing the social formation. This should not be seen, as it has been, as a denial of the role of political organisation or activity in bringing about the proletarian revolution, or as a juxtaposition of naked powerless individual and omnipotent historical process. Rather, it is the argument that there is no such thing as the individual as such, but that each mode of production produces its own mode of individuality in accordance with its specific character. Of course, the process whereby the particular mode of individuality is formed and maintained is the same process as that in which the mode of production becomes dominant in a particular social formation and is reproduced, and is one in which individuals take part, but again as the bearers, as Althusser puts it, of a given social formation. In the process of forming the agents of a mode of production, ideology plays a vital role:

> Every human, that is to say social individual, cannot be the agent of a practice unless he takes *the form of a subject*. The 'subject form' is in fact the form that the historical existence of every individual, every agent of social practices, takes: for the relations of production and reproduction necessarily involve, as the *integrating* element, what Lenin called '[*juridico-*]*ideological social relations*', which, in order to function, impose on every individual-agent the form of a *subject*.[80]

Thus the concept of history as a process without a subject and the theory of ideology find their connection in the idea that ideology is the way in which men and women are formed in order to participate in a process of which they are not the makers, and that ideology performs this function by giving them the illusion that history was made *for* them.

What does the conception of the dialectic summed up in the

phrase 'the process without a subject' leave us with? Centrally, with the idea of the *class struggle*. History is not the working out of some plan imprinted in the nature of man. It is the result of the struggles between different and opposed classes. These struggles are historically determined and conditioned, but history leaves their result open. There is no natural necessity à la Kautsky which decides which class will be victorious. The overthrow of capitalism and the construction of communism will be the work of the proletariat itself; if it does not win the class battle the prize will go to capital in its most barbarous forms. Althusser's chief achievement is to produce a version of the dialectic according to which history is determined not *pre*determined. This is no small result when we consider that this is something for which Marxist philosophers have been groping since Kautsky and Plekhanov, the high priests of natural necessity, turned their backs on the international working class movement in 1914.

But is the price too high? Must we accept that men and women as the active agents of history are necessarily the prisoners of ideology? We will pursue this question in the rest of the essay.

3. Epistemological Blues

The Ontology of Practices

We have already encountered a deep contradiction within Althusser's epistemology. It is the contradiction between the assertion that the autonomy of theoretical practice involves a 'radical inwardness' such that there is no general criterion of the scientificity of theoretical practice but rather that each properly constituted science possesses its own, specific, criteria of scientific validity, and the definition of Marxist philosophy as the theory of theoretical practice, whose specific role consists precisely in applying such a general criterion through its analysis of the knowledge-effect.[1] This contradiction is itself a part of a more general problem inherent in Althusser's system. For, if Althusser has argued very effectively in favour of the relative autonomy of the sciences, he has failed completely to show wherein lies the relative character of this autonomy. On the one hand, theoretical practice is assimilated to those familiar constituents of the superstructure, politics and ideology, as one of the practices that, together with, and under the determination in the last instance of, the economy, form the social totality. On the other hand, any suggestion that the sciences are part of the superstructure is firmly rejected.[2]

Well, in the first place, although Althusser gives us good reason for accepting that the sciences are not part of the superstructure, it is impossible, in terms of both his conception of the social totality and his general definition of practice, to differentiate the position of theoretical practice from that on any other element of the superstructure. In order to make out his case, it would be incumbent upon Althusser to analyse the *differential* relation between theoretical practice and the rest of the social formation. This includes, not only its relation to the economy and the superstructure, but also its relation to the class struggle itself. We have already noted his derisory 'solution' to the problem of the unity of theory and practice.[3] This complete failure to confront the problem reflects a more generalised failure to deal with the problem of the relation of the sciences to the rest of the social totality.

I have suggested that this failure at least in part reflects the logic of the system itself. The uniform subsumption of both the sciences and the superstructure under the general heading of practices possessing a common structure and, for all one is told to the contrary, the same general position in the whole, gives Althusser very little room in which to manœuvre. This should lead us to reflect on the general role that the definition of practice plays in Althusser's system. We shall find that, despite the appearance that its role consists essentially of a specification of the nature of the Marxist dialectic, in fact the most important part it has to play is an *epistemological* one.

I have already referred to the existence of a circle at the heart of Althusser's philosophy.[4] We shall see that it is precisely the notion of practice that is the condition of this circle's possibility. Althusser explicitly admits this.

> May I sum up all this in a sentence. This sentence describes a circle: a philosophical reading of *Capital* is only possible as the application of that which is the very object of our investigation, Marxist philosophy. This circle is only epistemologically possible because of the existence of Marx's philosophy in the works of Marxism. It is therefore a question of producing, in the precise sense of the word, which seems to signify making manifest what is latent, but really means transforming . . . something which in a sense *already exists*. This production, in the double sense which gives the production operation the necessary form of a circle, is the *production of a knowledge*. To conceive Marx's philosophy in its specificity is therefore to conceive the essence of the very movement with which the knowledge of it is produced, or to conceive of knowledge as production.[5]

As we have seen, the notion of production, of a work of transformation of a raw material into a finished product, is at the heart of Althusser's definition of practice. Althusser is here employing the concept of production to guarantee the epistemological validity of his own work.

The problem is one created by Althusser's definition of his project: to extract the principles of Marxist philosophy from Marx's work by applying to it *Marxist philosophy itself*. This operation is rendered possible thanks to the status of Marxist philosophy itself. Marxist philosophy is the theory of theoretical practice: its object is the production of knowledges. As such, its emergence was involved in the emergence in 1845 of the science of social formations, whose object is the production of the 'society-effect'.[6] Thus Althusser writes:

> [But] the circle implied in this operation is, like all circles of this kind, simply the dialectical circle of the question asked of an object as to its nature, on the basis of a theoretical problematic which in putting its object to the test puts itself to the test of its object. That Marxism can and must itself be the object of the epistemological question, that the epistemological question can only be asked as a function of the Marxist theoretical problematic, that is necessity itself for a theory which defines itself dialectically, not merely as a science of history (historical materialism) but also simultaneously as a philosophy that is capable of accounting for the nature of theoretical formations and their history, and therefore *capable of accounting for itself*, by taking itself as its own object. Marxism is the only philosophy that theoretically faces up to this test.[7]

So what is in question is a theoretical work of production on the part of the theory of theoretical practice, that of explaining its own production by a reading of the works in which it emerged, works which are devoted to the inauguration of a new science, historical materialism. At least the structure of the operation in question seems clear. Yet a number of problems remain. If the mechanism of the epistemological break appeared mysterious,[8] more mysterious still is the fact that this break involved the covert emergence of a distinct theory, Marxist philosophy, the theory of theoretical practice. If the problematic of Marxist science required a symptomatic reading for it to be extracted from Marx's texts, how much more so will the problematic of Marxist philosophy, whose principles in some strange ('dialectical') form are present in these same texts. Yet, since the notions of symptomatic reading and problematic are categories of Marxist philosophy, how do we come to possess these albeit provisional principles of Marxist philosophy, since they are necessary in order to initiate the circular motion described by Althusser's work?

Althusser at one point gives us an answer:

This critical reading [of *Capital*] seems to constitute a circle, since we appear to be expecting to obtain Marxist philosophy from its own application. We should therefore clarify: we expect from *theoretical work* of the philosophical principles Marx has explicitly given us or which can be disengaged from his Works of the Break and Transitional Works[9] – we can expect from the *theoretical work* of these principles applied to *Capital* their development and enrichment as well as refinements in their rigour. This apparent circle should not surprise us: all 'production' of knowledge implies it in its process.[10]

Now, this will not do at all. It simply shifts the problem: what are the principles according to which a correct reading of the Works of the Break and the Transition should take place? Or do we have a case here of an innocent reading? If so, not only is Althusser violating his own principles, he is also performing a manœuvre that he has already condemned as a mere evasion. By loading on to an *original reading* of Marx's philosophical writings a self-evidence which serves to cover all the problems that he is unable to solve within his system, he is invoking the familiar philosophical concept of *origin*, whose function, as he says shortly before the above passage, 'is to summarise in one word what has not to be thought in order to be able to think what one wants to think'.[11]

It is not, however, strictly accurate to say that Althusser cannot solve these problems within his system. For we have seen in his comments on the circle, repeated each time, a final comfort for the unconvinced: all knowledge takes the form of a production. By invoking the magical word 'production' Althusser seeks to prevent his system from collapsing. This is rendered possible by the common characterisation, in the general definition of practice, of both theoretical practice and the other instances of the social formation. Marxist philosophy is strictly defined as the theory of theoretical practice. It bears no relation to any other practice. It is therefore possible for it to operate in complete independence of everything beyond theory. And the epistemological validity of its work on and in theory is secured by the fact that it too is a theory, it too produces knowledges, it too possesses the form of a production, similar in structure to that of theoretical practice itself.

Philosophy, dialectical materialism, is assimilated to science. However, it is a science of a special sort, enjoying a peculiar, privileged status, which enables it, once spontaneously generated in a birth that defies comprehension, to account for its own mysterious origins.

This position of privilege derives in the last instance from the more general epistemological role that the theory of theoretical practice plays within Althusser's system. This is what Althusser says of dialectical materialism:

> The *relation* of a 'theory' to its practice . . . is also relevant to the general theory (the dialectic) in which is theoretically expressed the essence of theoretical practice in general, through it the essence of practice in general, and through it the essence of the transformations, of the 'development' of things in general.[12]

Thus through philosophy is expressed not only the cognitive relation between theoretical practice and the other social practices, that is, between historical materialism and its real object, social formations, but also the relation, mediated by these practices, *between thought and reality as such.* How is this possible? 'Through the essence of the transformations' – that is, *by virtue of the common structure of all practices.*

Now, in the first place, there is no earthly reason why the structure of social practice should tell us anything about the structure of the natural world, beyond its amenability to being worked upon by human labour. Indeed, this claim would seem to violate Althusser's thesis of the autonomy of the sciences: rather than producing valid knowledges of nature through their own specific and autonomous practices, it would seem that sciences like physics derive their validity from the relation between labour and nature reflected in the structure of social practice. But, more seriously, the role the theory of theoretical practice plays in Althusser's system involves a relapse into the bourgeois empiricist epistemology he has so vigorously criticised. For Althusser can now resolve the problem of scientificity: theoretical practice can cognitively appropriate its real object despite the fact that it takes place completely in thought because thought and the real are homologous – *they possess an identical structure, that of practice.* This solution follows from the position accorded to philosophy.[13]

Ironically enough, Althusser had criticised Colletti for precisely this same manœuvre of assimilating the structure of thought and the structure of the real.[14] Quite rightly: for to employ an asserted homology between thought and the real as the foundation for an epistemological position, is to fall into the empiricist problematic. Althusser has been able to produce a guarantee that science can appropriate the real, by means of a pre-existing relation existing between thought and reality – that of possessing identical structures. This solution is not that far removed from that of Engels in his *Dialectics of Nature*.

The effects of this position are clear-cut. Above all, it becomes impossible to avoid idealism. To assert the autonomy of theoretical practice without establishing the specific character of the relation it enjoys with the social whole, is to transform the sciences into an instance above and cut off from the social process. This unquestionably is the result of an epistemology according to which the relation of theory to the other social practices rests purely on their common structure, and the preservation intact of this relation is the prerogative of a philosophy whose only relation beyond itself is with the sciences. From the standpoint of Marxism, it is clearly a position that must be rejected. Otherwise, Marxism would become a theory lacking in any actuality beyond the theoretician's cabinet, any relation to the life and struggle of the proletariat.[15]

Philosophy and the Class Struggle

It would seem, then, that we must dismiss Althusser's position as idealist and incoherent. But, the second adjective, 'incoherent', reminds us that much the best critique of Althusser's position derives from his own work, or at least certain aspects of it. Althusser's critique of empiricist epistemology is a powerful and persuasive one, and it is from the standpoint of this critique that I have developed my own criticisms of his assimilation of thought and reality via the definition of practice in general. Now, this critique of epistemology, including, as it turns out, his own, might serve as the kernel of a radically new philosophical position. And, indeed, such a position does exist, developed by Althusser himself, in various recent texts, most notably perhaps *Lenin and Philosophy* and *Reply to John Lewis*.

For Althusser became sufficiently aware of the contradictions in his position to attempt to confront and resolve them. In *To My English Readers*, written in 1967 and published in the English edition of *For Marx*, he criticises himself on two grounds. Firstly, he 'did not enter into the question of the unity of theory and practice within *political practice*'; hence what he describes as 'theoreticist' readings of his essays. Secondly, he 'left vague the difference distinguishing philosophy from science'; hence positivist readings of his essays (positivism can be defined for present purposes as the assimilation of philosophy to science).[16] In the Foreword to the Italian edition of *Reading Capital*, which appeared in 1968, he identifies the source of these errors as the definition he had made of philosophy:

> The definition of philosophy as a *theory of theoretical practice* . . . is unilateral and therefore inaccurate . . . To define philosophy in a unilateral way as the Theory of theoretical practice (and in consequence as a theory of the differences between the practices) is a formulation that could not help but induce either 'speculative' or 'positivist' theoretical effects and echoes.[17]

The unilateralism of the definition lies, as we shall see, in its failure to express philosophy's relation to the class struggle.

In *Lenin and Philosophy* Althusser attacks what he has come to see as the source of his previous errors – the definition of philosophy. He does so on the basis of a reading of Lenin's *Materialism and Empirio-Criticism*. His starting point is a rejection of any assimilation of philosophy and the sciences: 'Philosophy is not a science. Philosophy is distinct from the sciences. Philosophical categories are distinct from scientific concepts.'[18] This involves a denial of the essentially identical structure and functioning of philosophy and the sciences on the old definition. It does not follow that there is no relation between philosophy and the sciences. On the contrary: 'If philosophy is distinct from the sciences, there is a privileged link between philosophy and the sciences. The link is represented by the materialist thesis of objectivity.'[19]

In fact, the materialist thesis of objectivity involves two theses: firstly, the primacy of being over thought, and, secondly, the objectivity of knowledges. It could be summed up as the assertion that the sciences involve the objective reflection of the real in thought. The link between the sciences and philosophy consists in the fact that philosophical discourse is structured by the two materialist theses I have outlined – philosophy must be seen in terms of the positions taken by different philosophical tendencies in relation to these theses. Philosophers are to be classified in accordance with whether they reject or accept these theses and which order they place them in (thus to discuss the second thesis, that of the objectivity of the sciences, save on the basis of an assertion of the primacy of being over thought, would be to fall into agnosticism, which is a form of idealism). The number of philosophical tendencies under this classification reduces to two: materialism and idealism. To stop short of acceptance of both theses would be to fall into some version of idealism.

Lenin's philosophical practice in *Materialism and Empirio-Criticism* is taken as an example. Lenin is arguing against those idealist philosophers like Ernst Mach who exploited the crisis that physics found itself in at the turn of the century and which resulted in the emergence of relativity theory and quantum mechanics, new theories of the structure of matter, to claim that because a particular theory of the structure of matter (classical physics) had collapsed, therefore materialism had collapsed and it would no longer be possible to maintain the separation of thought and reality that materialism implied. In doing so, Lenin championed the sciences by defending the materialist thesis of objectivity and asserted the distinctness of philosophical categories, which relate essentially to these theses, and scientific concepts, which are constructed in order to produce knowledges, and which therefore may be replaced by other concepts in the continual process of development of the sciences. Thus:

> It is absolutely unpardonable to confuse, as the Machists do, any particular theory of the structure of matter with the epistemological category, to confuse the problem of the new properties of new aspects of matter (electrons, for example) with the old problem of the theory of knowledge, with the problem of the sources of our knowledge, the existence of objective truth, etc . . . Matter is a philosophical category denoting the objective reality which is given to man by his sensations, and which is copied, photographed and reflected by our sensations, while existing independently of them.[20]

79

And:

> From the standpoint of modern materialism, i.e. Marxism, the *limits* of the approximation of our knowledge to objective, absolute truth are historically conditional, but the existence of such truth is *unconditional*, and the fact that we are approaching nearer to it is unconditional.[21]

Althusser does not, however, limit himself to this redefinition of the relation between philosophy and the sciences. He also argues that philosophy's role in theory is a very special one. It consists not in the knowledges that are produced by the work of philosophy on some theoretical object, some Generality I, for philosophy has no object, but in certain practical effects: in the case of materialism, the effect is one of demarcating between the scientific and the non-scientific:

> Lenin . . . defines the ultimate essence of philosophical practice as an *intervention* in the theoretical domain. This intervention takes a double form: it is theoretical in its formulation of definite categories; and practical in the function of these categories. This function consists in 'drawing in a dividing line' inside the theoretical domain between ideas declared to be true and ideas declared to be false, between the scientific and the ideological. The effects of this line are of two kinds: positive in that they assist a certain practice – scientific practice – and negative in that they defend this practice against the dangers of certain ideological notions: here those of idealism and dogmatism.[22]

Thus philosophy, far from being the instance which provides the science with the guarantee of their validity, becomes a practice, which, at best, can serve to defend already constituted sciences with their own, specific, internal criteria of validity, against the encroachments of ideology.

But in whose name does philosophy make its intervention in the theoretical domain? It is at this point that the radicalism of Althusser's new definition of philosophy emerges: 'Philosophy is, in the last instance, the class struggle in theory.'[23] The materialist and idealist positions taken up in philosophy reflects in the last instance, the class positions the philosophers represent. If vulgar materialism reflected the class position of the revolutionary bourgeoisie, dialectical materialism represents that of the revolutionary proletariat.

This thesis should not be seen as any sort of crude reduction of philosophy to politics. Rather, it is the assertion that the positions taken up in relation to the materialist theses, and in relation to the scientific or unscientific character of particular theories, is determined in the last instance by the interests of the different classes, and ultimately reflect these interests:

> Philosophy is a certain continuation of politics, in a certain domain, *vis-à-vis* a certain reality. Philosophy represents politics in the domain of theory, or to be more precise; *with the sciences* – and *vice versa*, philosophy represents scientificity in politics, with the classes engaged in the class struggle.[24]

Thus, one could argue that Karl Popper's attempt to demarcate science from pseudo-science, and to include historical materialism and psychoanalysis in the latter category, was determined in the last instance by the bourgeoisie's political need to deny these sciences any objective validity, since they presented a massive threat to bourgeois ideology.[25] The novelty of Marxist philosophy with respect to all previous philosophy is that, while all previous philosophy, in keeping with its ideological role, *denegated* its reality, denying that philosophy had any connection with politics while nonetheless continuing to practice politics in its theoretical interventions, Marxist philosophy openly admits its political nature, as Lenin's notion of partisanship in philosophy implies.

Probably the best way to come to grips with the new definition of philosophy is to look at its implications. Althusser states that they are twofold.

1. It is impossible to reduce philosophy to science, Marx's philosophical revolution to the 'epistemological break'.
2. Marx's philosophical revolution necessitated the 'epistemological break', as one of its conditions of possibility.[26]

We have already encountered the first point, in the form of a rejection of any assimilation of philosophy to science. We have seen its importance, in ruling out the erection of philosophy into a Science of Sciences that is the guarantor of the epistemological validity of the sciences.[27] This should not, on the other hand, be seen as a positivist reduction of philosophy to nonsense (or to the laws of pure thought, as in the case of Hume and, regrettably, Engels). Philosophy has a role to play in relation to the sciences, but a strictly limited one. Althusser puts forward a general thesis to the effect that each major epistemological break involves a philosophical revolution, which demarcates the theory from the pre-existing ideologies by articulating its problematic. According to him, there have been three such breaks, each of which opened up a new 'Continent' to science. Firstly, there was the development of mathematics in antiquity by the Greeks. This involved the emergence of the first properly philosophical discourse – that of Plato – in which certain problems that had arisen in mathematics (e.g. the discovery of irrational numbers) were thought out.[28] The second great epistemological break was the inauguration of a scientific physics in the work of Galileo, which involved both a resort to Platonist philosophy in order to think the break with Aristotelian physics, and the development in the philosophical work of Descartes of the categories necessary for the articulation of the new problematic.[29]

Finally, there was of course the inauguration by Marx of the science of history. Once again, this involved a philosophical revolution, which we will discuss in detail below. Here it is chiefly necessary to emphasise that this philosophical revolution is not reducible to the epistemological break. In his earlier writings, Althusser had assimilated the two, with the result that the epistemological break was held to have spontaneously – and mysteriously – generated a philosophical revolution. This led to a failure to take sufficient account in Marx's post-1845 work of concepts and terminology that reflect the presence in this work of *survivals* of his ideological past – e.g. the use of the term 'alienation' frequently in the *Grundrisse* and occasionally in *Capital*. According to Althusser, these survivals reflect the fact that the philosophical articulation of an epistemological break lags behind that break, and hence, pending this articulation, it would be no more surprising to find the presence of pre-scientific concepts in Marx's later writings, than it is to find, according to Koyré, that the correct formulation of the law of inertia discovered by Galileo had to wait upon the philosophical work of Descartes:[30]

82

If I have not been attentive to the *fact* to which J. Lewis has drawn attention, to the presence of these philosophical categories *after* the epistemological break, it is for a basically theoretical reason: because I identified the 'epistemological ($=scientific$) break' with Marx's *philosophical* revolution. More precisely, I thought the philosophical revolution as identical with the 'epistemological break'. I thus thought philosophy on the model of 'science' and logically wrote that in 1845 Marx operated a *double* scientific and philosophical 'break'.[31]

Unquestionably, however, the more important thesis is the second, that Marx's philosophical revolution was one of the preconditions of his epistemological break. It involves a reconsideration of the relationship between the sciences and the other instances of the social formation. This becomes clear in Althusser's revaluation of the nature of the epistemological break, above all in the essay, *The Conditions of Marx's Scientific Discovery*. The shift emerges in the discussion of ideology at the beginning of this essay, where the important feature of ideology for Althusser has become, not so much its epistemological character (i.e. that it is mystification), as its *social* role in the class struggle:

> Ideologies are not illusions pure and simple (Error), but bodies of representations existing in institutions and practices: they feature in the superstructure and are based on the class struggle. If the science founded by Marx makes the theoretical conceptions inscribed in its own prehistory appear as ideological, it is therefore not just in order to denounce it as false: it is also in order to say that they present themselves as true and were and still are accepted as true -- and in order to provide the reasons for this necessity. . . .
>
> If this is so, the 'break' between Marxist science and its ideological prehistory refers us to something quite different from a theory of the difference between science and ideology, to something quite different from an epistemology. It refers us on the one hand to a theory of the superstructure, in which feature the State and Ideologies. . . . It refers us on the other hand to a theory of the material conditions (production), the social conditions (division of labour), (class struggle), ideological conditions and philosophical conditions of the processes of production of knowledges. These two theories derive in the last instance from historical materialism.[32]

83

We can observe here the last step in Althusser's critique of epistemology, the rejection of all epistemology – that is to say, the rejection of any philosophical theory that involves the determination of the validity of scientific theories as knowledges. In its place we have, on the one hand, dialectical materialism, the class struggle of the revolutionary proletariat in theory, whose function is, as we have seen, not a cognitive one; and on the other hand, historical materialism, the science of history, whose function is limited to historical analyses of the development of the sciences both in their own autonomy and, for present purposes more significantly, in their relation to the social conditions of theoretical practice. This explodes the ontology of practices previously encountered in Althusser's work. The sciences, far from being an instance of the social formation of the same character as the economy and the superstructure, become an autonomous practice articulated upon the superstructure. This theoretical reorganisation is present in the essay on *Ideology and Ideological State Apparatuses*: the role of the superstructure is defined by its contribution to the reproduction of the social formation. Clearly, theoretical practice cannot be assimilated to the same plane as ideology and the state analysed in these terms. Its specificity can be defined in terms of, on the one hand, the mode of functioning of the sciences, their 'radical inwardness', and, on the other hand, their objective content, as affirmed by the materialist thesis of objectivity. However, theoretical practice is articulate upon the superstructure and materialised in the Ideological State Apparatuses – the universities, for example. This relation to the superstructure is reflected in the presence within the sciences of theoretical ideologies, theories whose structure is a function of their subordination to specific class interests, rather than to the interest of knowledge as such. This brings out clearly the necessity for a theory of the relation between the class struggle and theory.

Here of course we return to the new definition of philosophy, since, according to it, philosophy is the reflection in theory of the class struggle itself. Of course, such a theory would be part of a broader theory of the conditions of scientific practice, which would involve, as Althusser says, a theory of the material, social and ideological, as well as philosophical, conditions of the process of knowledge. We encounter intimations of such a theory in Althusser's discussion of the conditions of Marx's scientific discovery.

The starting point is historical materialism, its specificity, and the implications that this has for the conditions of its emergence and acceptance:

> This science cannot be a science like any other, a science for 'everyone'. Precisely because it reveals the mechanisms of class exploitation, repression and domination, in the economy, in politics, and in ideology, it cannot be recognised by *everyone*. This science, which brings the social classes face to face with their truth, is unbearable for the bourgeoisie and its allies, who reject it and take refuge in their so-called 'social sciences': it is only acceptable to the proletariat, who it 'represents' (Marx). That is why the proletariat has recognised it as its own property and set it to work in its practice: in the hands of the Workers' Movement, Marxist science has become the theoretical weapon of the revolution.[33]

Or, as he put it elsewhere:

> To understand *Capital* . . . it is necessary to take up 'proletarian class positions', i.e. to adopt the only viewpoint that renders *visible* the reality of the exploitation of wage labour power, which constitutes the whole of capitalism.[34]

But it is not simply a matter of the political position that is a precondition for a break with the ideological theories that mask the reality of the class struggle. This political position must be reflected *in theory*:

> It was by *moving over* to absolutely unprecedented proletarian theoretical class positions that Marx activated the effectivity of the theoretical conjunction from which emerged the Science of History.[35]

This can be seen in the development of Marx's thought. The works of the Young Marx record a progress *in philosophy* towards proletarian communism. The starting point is the radical-democratic political position found in Marx's writings in the *Rheinische Zeitung* in the early forties. In 1843 Marx adopted the cause of the revolutionary proletariat in the name of an avowedly communist materialism; this political shift is present in the *Introduction to the*

85

Contribution to a Critique of Hegel's Philosophy of Right. But it brought with it a theoretical crisis in the form of a contradiction between Marx's new political position and the petit-bourgeois humanist theoretical position he still held to. The *Manuscripts* of 1844 are an attempt to resolve this crisis, an attempt doomed from the start by the contradiction between the tendency in the *Manuscripts* to seek to determine the material conditions for both the present situation of the proletariat and the revolution that can end it, on the one hand, and the teleological structure of the dialectic functioning in that work, on the other. The resolution of the crisis presupposed a philosophical rejection of the humanist problematic and its replacement with concepts specifying the nature of history as a process without a subject. This came in 1845.

> It can be said that in this process [that of the development of Marx's thought – AC], in which the *object* occupies the forestage, it is the political (class) position that occupies the determinant place, but the philosophical position that occupies the central place, for it is the last that ensures the theoretical relationship between the political position and the object of reflection. This can be verified empirically in the history of the Young Marx. It was indeed politics that made him move from one object to the other (schematically: from Press laws to the State and then to political Economy), but each time this move was realised and expressed in the form of a new philosophical position. From one point of view the philosophical position seems to be the theoretical expression of the political (and ideological) position. From another, this translation of the political position into theory (in the form of a philosophical position) seems to be the condition of the theoretical relation to the object of reflection.
>
> If this is so, and if philosophy does indeed represent politics in theory, then it can be said that Marx's philosophical position represents, in its variations, the *theoretical class conditions* of his reflection. If this is so, it will come as no surprise that the rupture of 1845, which inaugurated the foundation of a new science, was first expressed in the form of a philosophical rupture, of a 'settling of accounts' with the erstwhile philosophical conscience, and beneath the proclamation of a philosophical position without precedent.[36]

Thus, far from being generated by the epistemological break,

Marx's philosophical revolution was a precondition for the epistemological break:

> It is not enough to adopt a proletarian *political* position. This political position must be elaborated into a theoretical (philosophical) position for what is visible from the standpoint of the proletariat to be conceived and thought in its causes and mechanisms. Without this *displacement*, the Science of History is unthinkable and impossible.[37]

The role of philosophy is that of the theoretical reflection of proletarian class positions. This definition enables us to think both the autonomy of theoretical practice and its relationship to the class struggle. In order for the problematic of historical materialism to emerge, it was necessary for its founders to take up a proletarian class position.[38] However, historical materialism was not automatically generated by the taking up of this position (see, for example, Marx's discussion of the Ricardian left, who took up proletarian political positions while remaining prisoners of the problematic of bourgeois political economy theoretically[39]). It required the reflection of this political position in theory, that is, philosophically, for the preconditions for the emergence of historical materialism to come into existence.

It is important in this context not to lose sight of the specificity of the sciences, and of the epistemological break, lest we make the opposite error to that of Althusser's earlier writings and collapse the epistemological break into the philosophical revolution. This would be to relapse into historicism. The development of historical materialism was an autonomous theoretical development, but one requiring the existence of certain conditions inside and outside theory, the former including a *prise de position*, the taking up of a proletarian political position in theory. This is not a condition whose necessity vanishes upon the foundation of historical materialism. On the contrary: 'This epistemological break is not an instantaneous event . . . [but rather] a sustained one within which complex reorganisations can be observed.'[40]

This process of development and reorganisation, combined with the articulation of the sciences upon the superstructure, carries with it a continual danger of the resurgence of ideology, either directly or by means of philosophy. Hence the need for the sort of philosophy that defends the sciences against the encroachments of ideology, the sort of philosophy practised by Lenin:

> There is a history of the sciences, and the lines of the philosophical front are displaced according to the transformations of the scientific conjuncture (i.e. according to the state of the sciences and their problems), and according to the state of the philosophical apparatuses that these transformations induce. The terms that designate the scientific and the ideological have to be *rethought* again and again.[41]

In concluding, I think we can see that Althusser has been able to rescue his system from an internal critique by abandoning the whole notion of epistemology. In the process, he has succeeded in producing the elements of a theory of the relation between the sciences and the class struggle, which captures both the autonomy of theoretical practice and the necessity for certain class conditions to be established in theory before a particular science can be constituted. He does so by means of a theory of philosophy, not as the Science of Sciences, but as the instance which, mediating between the sciences and politics, establishes these conditions. He thereby also provides us with a much clearer idea of the process whereby historical materialism emerged. For its completion, the theory requires the framework for a history of the Sciences that can account for developments within the sciences both as autonomous practices and as instances articulated upon the superstructure, and hence requiring certain material, social and ideological conditions for their operation.[42]

Here Althusser's work is at its strongest. The development from the idealist treatment of the sciences in *For Marx* and *Reading Capital* to the position I have discussed in this section represents, along with the concepts of overdetermination and conjuncture, Althusser's most important contribution to Marxist theory.

4. The Politics of Ambiguity

Althusser and the PCF – The Problem of Stalinism

If we accept Althusser's definition of philosophy as the class struggle in theory, then the logical next step would be to see what fruit this definition bears when applied to Althusser himself. I shall not attempt to do so in any detailed way, but will merely sketch out the main problems and then relate them to certain features of Althusser's theoretical position.

One problem in any discussion of Althusser's politics is that, until very recently, in his philosophical works there was no serious attempt by Althusser to relate his philosophical position to any coherently expounded political position, beyond assertions of Marxist orthodoxy that anyone could agree with and which could mean anything he cared them to mean. If we look at *For Marx*, beyond a few oblique references to the crimes of Stalin, there is nothing but a criticism of the unscientific nature of the concept of the cult of personality, which, while perfectly unexceptionable, is fairly unhelpful since it is not accompanied by any sort of alternative analysis. We are informed of the need for such an alternative, historical materialist, analysis of Stalinism, and are told that the concept of overdetermination will be of use here – but nothing more. Because we know that Althusser is a member of the French Communist Party, we can glean from this that he does not agree with the line of the PCF leadership, which is to paper over the contradictions in their criticism of Stalin by invoking the concept of the cult of personality, and also that he is critical of Stalin, so that it would be wrong to classify him as a dogmatic, hard-line Stalinist. But nothing more emerges.

We should remember that the problem of Stalinism is not a minor one for any Marxist. Whatever our interpretation may be, the reality of the phenomenon of Stalinism is undeniable: the transformation of the Bolshevik Party into a bureaucracy controlled through increasingly terroristic measures by its General Secretary, and that bureaucracy's transformation of Russia into an advanced industrial state capable of defeating Nazi Germany and conquering Eastern Europe at the price of the abolition of all remnants of socialist democracy, the massacre of millions of peasants, and savage repression against the working class. Its analysis is vital not simply because of its inherent significance – the fate of the first workers' state – but also because of its influence on outside events – because the dominance of the Russian party within the Comintern enabled the Stalinist bureaucracy to establish its regime in the other Communist Parties and thereby influence, uniformly for the worse, the fate of the revolution in other countries, for example, Germany and Spain in the 1930s.

For any Marxist, to account for this phenomenon and to deduce from this analysis conclusions about the tasks of revolutionaries, particularly in the Eastern bloc, is of the first importance. The significance this question assumed for the tendencies deriving from Trotsky's theoretical and political heritage is well-known. But those in the Communist Parties are not absolved from this task either. Indeed, precisely because these parties arise from the Stalinist tradition, the task is a more urgent one. Thus the presuppositions involved in analyses of the role the Communist Party ought to play today – the question of broad, popular alliances of anti-monopoly elements—are essentially those involved in the strategy of Popular Fronts against fascism adopted by the Seventh Congress of the Comintern in 1935 at Stalin's behest. These analyses deal with the most important question facing socialists – in Britain, for example, the line to be adopted towards Parliament and the Labour Party. In some cases, they deal with questions literally of life and death, as was true of Chile, and, perhaps, will be true of Portugal.

A concomitant, however, of the peculiar importance of a settling of accounts with Stalinism for the world Communist movement is its inability to achieve it. An index of this inability is the concept of the cult of personality, as if the abuse of power by one individual and his associates could explain a phenomenon of such world historic importance. The reasons for this inability vary. In the case of the Russian

Party they are fairly obvious. It has been necessary for the leadership to condemn the particular practices of Stalin while deflecting criticisms of the system as such, since it is essentially the same today as it was in Stalin's time. The concept of the cult of personality serves admirably to detach Stalin's 'abuse of socialist legality' from the conjuncture of which they were a part. It is thus possible to laud the 1930s as the period of the triumph of socialism in one country, while condemning some of the methods required to achieve this 'triumph'. The reasons for the condemnation of Stalin reflected both the socioeconomic pressures towards a reliance more on market mechanisms rather than direct repression in running the economy and the tendency that existed under Stalin's police state for the upper echelons of the bureaucracy to form a significant number of its victims. The extent of this de-Stalinisation should be clear, in the light of the persistent persecution of political dissidents and Jews under Brezhnev.

In the case of the Communist Parties in the West this is more complex. Since the war, the possession by the Russian bureaucracy of nuclear weapons has made reliance on the European parties far less necessary as an instrument of Soviet foreign policy. The resulting tendency for these parties to become transformed into classical reformist parties is well documented.[1] Hence the part that some Western parties, notably the Italian, have played in pushing for de-Stalinisation, and the virtual unanimity with which they condemned the Russian invasion of Czechoslovakia. But there are counteracting tendencies. The Communist Parties still derive a significant proportion of their support from a persisting image of socialist militancy that they project, in part thanks to an ideology in which the Soviet Union, as the first socialist country, plays a significant role. Any radical devaluation of the Soviet Union would threaten a severe crisis within the Communist Parties. Therefore, the question of Stalinism remains delicate, little troubled by any attention apart from the repetition of the Psalms in praise of the first socialist country and dewy-eyed reports of the triumphs of Soviet pig-iron forging or ballet-dancing, even in the case of parties which have proceeded particularly far along the reformist road, like the British.

We can see, therefore, the importance of Althusser's discussion of Stalinism for an understanding of his politics. Indeed, in *Reply to John Lewis*, particularly the French edition, where Althusser discusses the politics of his philosophical intervention, the question of Stalinism and the crisis which has been its heritage for the post-war Communist movement, play a central role. Yet this text also is infested with ambiguity.

The essentials of the argument seem to be as follows. Althusser's philosophical intervention has been aimed against the couple economism/humanism. The former consists in the reduction of all other instances of the social formation to epiphenomena of the economy, and, consequently, in a politics which relies upon an economic deus ex machina to produce the proletarian revolution. Humanism interprets history as the drama of a Subject, man, his alienation and necessary reconciliation, thus suppressing the reality of history as a process whose motor is the class struggle, and obscuring the lines that have to be drawn between classes with different interests in the political struggle if the proletariat is to take power. Both economism and humanism are closely related, above all in the Hegelian problematic, whose concept of totality reduces its instances to expressions of its essence, and whose dialectic is essentially a teleological one. Humanism has been a dominant characteristic of those tendencies in the Communist camp which have championed de-Stalinisation while using the cult of personality as a way of evading a settling of accounts, theoretical and political, with Stalin. Economism, on the other hand, was, according to Althusser the chief feature of what he calls the Stalinist 'deviation'.

This would seem to set the stage for Althusser's critique of Stalinism (although his describing it as a 'deviation', a mere political error rather than the socio-historic phenomenon that it was and is, is a bad sign). However, even here we are in for a disappointment. After a repetition of the criticisms of the cult of personality for abstracting from the role of the party and the state, the mode of production and the class struggle, etc. we are informed that there is such a thing as a right critique of Stalinism and a left critique of Stalinism. Under the former heading are found, not only the studies of 'totalitarianism' beloved of American political scientists, but also the analyses of Russia produced by Trotskyists. Now, *a priori*, this may seem a bit strange, to classify some of the most serious attempts, albeit often faulty ones, to produce a Marxist analysis of the Russian social formation, without bothering to characterise or argue against them.

We are informed that Trotskyism is unworthy of our attention since it can claim no great historic victory for its cause. For a Trotskyist to give this remark the reply it deserves, he need simply point out that the organisation of the October insurrection and the foundation of the Red Army were not minor achievements, or that compared to such historic victories of Stalinist politics as the triumph of Nazism in Germany or of Franco in Spain most defeats would pale. We can certainly say that Althusser's observation is not a serious argument against another Marxist tendency (he could of course expel the Trotskyists from the Marxist tradition, as Stalin did when he classified – and shot – them as fascists), specially since a number of Althusser's followers have begun to play with the notion that the Russian social formation is state capitalist rather than socialist. To take the most notable case, Etienne Balibar, one of Althusser's collaborators in *Reading Capital*, has since worked with the economist Charles Bettelheim in his investigations of Russian society, which conclude that state capitalism is that society's dominant feature.[2]

Althusser, after his dismissal of Trotskyism, informs us that there is also a left critique of the Stalinist 'deviation' implicit in the practice of the Chinese Revolution, from the Long March to the Cultural Revolution. We are not told what this critique is, beyond some references, common in Althusser's recent writings, to the need for a correct 'mass line' on the part of the party. This should come as no surprise since this critique of Stalinism had remained so implicit as not to have come to the attention of the Chinese Communist Party, which is under the illusion that it is loyal to Stalin's memory. Indeed, it is unclear as to what this critique could pertain, since we are told that Stalin's positive achievements include the strategy of socialism in one country and the industrialisation in the thirties, despite the fact that preconditions for this industrialisation were savage labour laws, collectivisation and the massacre of millions of peasants and that a major aim of the Purges was the elimination of those Communists critical of collectivisation. But perhaps my criticisms are too crudely concrete to avoid the accusation of empiricism. . . .

The ambiguity we encountered in *For Marx* on the question of Stalinism is, in fact, a structural feature of Althusser's political position. Essentially, he is interested in an alternative to either the mere reaffirmation of Stalinism or the straightforward adoption of reformism. Yet, he is attempting to find one while remaining within a Stalinist problematic. By this I mean that he continues to accord validity to the main product of Stalinist rule, which was not, *pace* Solzhenitsyn, the terror, important though that was in the transformation of Russian society, but the creation of an advanced capitalist economy in Russia, albeit not one exploited by individual capitalists but by a state bureaucracy.[3] The problem of Stalinism for Communists is that of criticising certain of Stalin's practices while recognising his achievements in the construction of 'socialism' in Russia. This has tended to polarise between liberals and hardliners in both East and West, since Stalinism involves not only questions of historical analysis but also concrete political problems.

Althusser wishes to transcend this dichotomy, yet since he is unwilling to reject Stalin's achievement, or at least to permit the application of Marxist concepts to the Russian social formation as a whole, he is prevented from doing so. All he can do is refer obliquely to a Maoist 'left' critique, which presumably would concentrate on superstructural elements like the need for a cultural revolution (and a People's Liberation Army to put down the masses when they get out of hand, as they did in Shanghai in 1967), while evading the broader questions which even some of his followers are beginning to raise. One of the most interesting and important phenomena of recent years has been the evolution of certain Maoist tendencies in the West towards both a serious orientation towards the working class in their own countries, rather than the mixture of romantic Third Worldism and ultra-left voluntarism so well depicted in Godard's *La Chinoise*, and a critique of Stalinism that involves a class analysis of Russia. Althusser's Maoism, on the other hand, serves merely as a certificate of revolutionary militancy that enables him to evade the real questions that are Stalin's heritage.

94

This is not a purely theoretical matter (if such exists). Although illness prevented Althusser from any involvement in the events of May and June 1968 in France, we possess an analysis by him of these events in a letter he wrote to the Italian Communist, Maria Antonietta Macchiocchi. It is a sad document for those who respect Althusser's contribution to Marxist theory. All the usual intellectual machinery to produce a fact of the most stunning obviousness – that the most significant feature of these events was not the student revolt but the general strike. The implication of this banal pronouncement is that the revolutionary *groupuscules* were wrong to have criticised the PCF for failing to sense revolutionary possibilities in the situation. The different levels of consciousness of the workers and the students is cited as evidence for this claim. Apparently, the famous 'mass line' does not admit the possibility of a revolutionary party taking advantage of a favourable turn of events (presumably the largest general strike in history would fail under this heading) to raise the consciousness of the working class and develop the situation in the direction of revolution. To quote a contemporary analysis of the French events:

> The main condemnation of the PCF is not that they did not carry out a victorious socialist revolution in May or June. No one could have guaranteed that this could be done. What was necessary was to raise the self-confidence and organisational strength of the working class.
>
> The PCF prevented the election of democratic strike committees. It prevented the link-up between committees. It sent the majority of workers away from the factory. Those who were left were engaged in games instead of in serious political discussion. It did its best to insulate the workers from the revolutionary students and young workers. . . .
>
> The accusation against the PCF is not that it did not win an assault on the citadels of capitalism, but that it prevented anyone from even starting the assault.[4]

Thus despite the appearance of maintaining a critical distance between himself and the line of the leadership of the PCF, on the most important and fundamental political question since the war, Althusser returned meekly to the fold.

Ideology and the State

It would be a violation of Althusser's method if we were not to seek to trace the reflections of the ambiguities of his political position in his theory. One such reflection should be clear. We have already noted the way in which the definition of philosophy as the theory of theoretical practice serves to separate Marxism into Pure Reason above the class struggle and we can also note the way in which this definition serves to validate Althusser's own political practice, or lack thereof. Similarly, his neglect of the problem of the unity of theory and practice is symptomatic. Despite his self-criticism for this failure, his recent writings contain very little discussion of the problem, beyond vague references to the world-historic importance of the union of Marxism and the workers' movement, as if, despite his disclaimers, this union were something achieved once and for all. I shall return to this in the Conclusion of this essay.

The ambiguities of Althusser's political position are reflected, however, primarily in his theory of ideology and the state. It is this that has been subjected to the most sustained and effective criticism, most notably by Jacques Rancière, one of the collaborators in the original edition of *Reading Capital*, who has since broken with Althusser.[5] One of his major criticisms, the purely epistemological role that ideology plays in Althusser's theory, as one of the terms of the science/ideology opposition, rather than as one of the principal sites and determinants of the class struggle, while quite correct, has to some extent been deflected by Althusser's development of the theory of ideology by means of the notion of the Ideological State Apparatuses and his revision of his definition of philosophy.[6] However, there are certain general features of the theory of ideology which have not changed.

Above all, Althusser denies that ideology is something specific to class societies: '*Ideology is as such an organic part of every social totality.*'[7] We are given very little indication of why this should be so beyond the assertion that '*Ideology (as a system of mass represen- tations) is indispensable in any society if men are to be formed, transformed and equipped to respond to their conditions of ex- istence.*'[8] Ideology, the process whereby men's experience of their relation to the world is transformed by their insertion into a subject-object relation, is essential to the reproduction of every social formation.

Let us look closely at the claim before deciding what to make of it. Now, it is true that in any society we can expect men to possess a particular conception of the world, since every human activity is not automatic and mechanical but requires conscious and unconscious thought and choice. Hence, as Gramsci put it:

> Everyone is a philosopher, though in his own way and unconsciously, since even in the slightest manifestation of any activity whatever, in 'language' there is contained a specific conception of the world.[9]

It is also true that the process whereby such conceptions are formed will reflect the nature and demands of the particular relations of production in which men are inserted, rather than the choices and dramas of individual men. This will be the case also under communism, although the process will surely be a radically different one from that in class societies, since it will be one reflecting the management of production by the associated producers rather than the appropriation of the surplus by an exploiting class. Yet, it does not follow that the conceptions of the world of men in communist society will necessarily express the sort of imaginary relation to the world that ideology does on Althusser's account.

It is true that, if we accept Althusser's analysis of the sciences, such conceptions of the world will not have the character of sciences, since, as we have seen, the sciences are very specific practices, involving the employment of highly abstract concepts in accordance with norms specific to each science. However, since communism will involve the abolition of the distinction between intellectual and manual labour, we can expect a much wider participation in theoretical practice than under capitalism and hence a much broader diffusion of scientific concepts among the masses, including their presence in the conceptions of the world that govern practice.

Further, Althusser's theory of ideology is closely connected to Marx's analysis of fetishism in *Capital*. We have already discussed this analysis, and the way in which it produces appearances with an objective status through their role in the process of reproduction of capitalism.[10] However, there is an obverse to this coin. It is this. Marx's theory of fetishism is one specific to the capitalist mode of production. The fetishised appearance of things under capitalism derives ultimately from the nature of the commodity, in which the social character of labour is only established by means of the exchange of its products on the market. Now, it may be, as Balibar argues, that there are types of fetishism in other modes of production.[11] It would, however, be necessary to follow Marx in deriving their necessity from an analysis of the specific nature of the mode of production concerned. This is quite a different matter from a general assertion about the needs of 'society' as such, which is Althusser's method of argument.

Moreover, when Marx, as he sometimes does in *Capital*, contrasts the capitalist and communist modes of production, he implies fairly clearly that with the abolition of the production of commodities, and therefore of the mechanisms necessary for the existence of a mode of production based on generalised commodity production, the necessity for the fetishised appearance of the system will vanish. Thus, in discussing the fetishism of commodities, he writes:

> Let us now picture to ourselves . . . a community of free individuals, carrying on their work with the means of production in common, in which the labour power of all the different individuals is consciously applied as the combined labour power of the community. . . . The social relations of the individual producers, with regard both to their labour and to its products, are in this case perfectly simple and intelligible and that with regard not only to production but also to distribution.[12]

Rather than requiring the mystifying and anarchic mechanism of the market in order that society may be reproduced, production will be directly regulated and controlled by the producers in accordance with a consciously and collectively arrived at plan.

Recently, Balibar has sought to detach Althusser's theory from its dependence on Marx's analysis of fetishism, which he criticises as idealist, by emphasising the importance of the Ideological State Apparatuses for securing the dominance of ruling-class ideology, rather than any sort of automatic process directly generated by the relations of production themselves.[13] Undoubtedly, the integration of the theory of ideology with the theory of the state, and their mutual subordination to a theory of the non-economic conditions for the reproduction of the mode of production are an important development and one that provides a useful conceptual framework for a continuation of Gramsci's investigations of ideology and the state. Moreover, the thesis that the category of the subject is constitutive of all ideology is worth pursuing, as a provisional hypothesis at least. Problems, however, remain.[14] Indeed, the central problem of the justification of Althusser's hypostatisation of ideology takes on an even more acute form. For, the Marxist theory of the state involves not merely a theory of the state but also of the conditions for its abolition. The definition of the state as a machine of class repression is one specific to class societies, and the seizure of power by the proletariat is the first step in its abolition. If ideology is materialised in institutions that are part of the state apparatus, their role in the process in which the state is abolished is a very problematical one on Althusser's account. The natural solution would be to extend the theory of ideology into a theory that, like that of the state, determines both its conditions of existence and the conditions of its abolition.

This conclusion is one to which we are led by the Marxist tradition. Ideology as a system of representations that mystifies the relation between men and their conditions of existence is clearly, in the works of Marx, Engels and Lenin, the product of a class society. There it is essentially a means by which the ruling class maintains its position by obscuring the conditions of exploitation and oppression at the heart of society. The working class's need for such an ideology does not exist, since its interests lie in the abolition of all class society. It is for this reason also that, as Althusser argues, the science of social formations, which reveals the mechanisms of class exploitation and oppression, is one that involves as its precondition the taking up of a proletarian political position, and that it is this science that guides the proletariat in its struggle for political power.

The reasons for Althusser's continued refusal to thus transform his theory of ideology reflect a survival from his earlier work. There, as Rancière points out, the function of ideology is an epistemological one – that of providing a contrast to science:

The functioning of the 'Science/Ideology' opposition depends on the re-establishment of a space homologous to that which the whole metaphysical tradition assumes by opposing Science to its Other; thus supposing the closure of a universe of discourse divided into the realms of the true and the false, into the world of Science and that of its Other (opinion, error, illusion, etc.). If one fails to grasp that ideology is fundamentally the site of a struggle, of a class struggle, it immediately slips into this place determined by the history of metaphysics: the place of the Other of Science.[15]

The implication of an end of ideology thus conceived would be a return to a philosophical position which Althusser had already rejected – that of conceiving the essence of the real as immediately present in the appearances.[16] Communism would become the point at which history became transparent, the appearances the direct expression of the real, the resolution of the human drama in the complicity of subject and object. Yet, this need not follow from the adoption of the theory of the end of ideology, providing ideology is conceived, not as illusion to science's truth, but as a site of the class struggle. The complexity of the object of historical materialism, of the social formation, arises from its material nature and therefore would remain under communism. Even if the superstructure were abolished, the process of production itself would be a complex structure, involving a combination of distinct instances. Further, the necessity of science (*pace* Marx) is not dependent upon the existence of ideology, but derives rather from the nature of theoretical practice as an autonomous process in which knowledges are produced according to the specific norms and protocols of the sciences. The concept of the communist mode of production would be a complex one, requiring its construction in historical materialism, not one that arises spontaneously from the historical process.

There remains, therefore, a contradiction in Althusser's work. It derives from the juxtaposition of his altered theory of ideology, which sees ideologies as the site of class struggles and the reflections of class interest, rather than as the illusions that precede the Truth of Science, and his rejection of any form of epistemology, on the one hand, and the assertion that ideology is necessary to any society, on the other. This

100

results from a survival from his previous position, an epistemological conception of ideology. Whatever its causes, its result is to undermine the conception of Marxism as the theory of the class struggle (which Althusser champions in *Reply to John Lewis*) and to transform it into a sociology, a theory of the general conditions of social cohesion. As Rancière puts it:

> How, after having proclaimed that the whole of history is that of the class struggle, can it define functions like: *securing social cohesion in general*? Isn't it precisely because Marxism has nothing to say on this subject, that we have shifted our ground and moved on to that of a Comtean or Durkheimian type sociology, which actually does concern itself with the systems of representations that secure or break up the cohesion of the social group?[17]

This may be no more than a tendency in Althusser's work, but it is one with serious political consequences. For the notion that the masses necessarily live in ideology, and that it will therefore be necessary for there to continue to exist a group of those adept in the sciences in order to guide them, derives from this position. Thus conceived, the theory of ideology can serve as a justification for bureaucratic state capitalism in the Eastern bloc. For, there, it is of course true that ideology (and the state) persist and indeed flourish, with a consequent need for an explanation of this fact that does not challenge these countries' claim to be socialist. Moreover, it serves to provide theoreticians with an excuse for separating themselves from the class struggle, to pursue the needs of pure theory far from the ideology-steeped class struggle. In these circumstances, the thesis that philosophy is the class struggle in theory can serve as an alibi for political immobilism.

Conclusion

No summing up on Althusser could be adequate without taking into account the complex and contradictory character of his work. We can see in restrospect the extent to which Althusser's work is structured by the tension between his rejection of epistemology, of any theory of guarantees, of the difference between science and non-science, truth and illusion, and the presence of epistemological categories in his work. In his best-known writings, *For Marx* and *Reading Capital*, this resulted in a conception of philosophy as the theory of theoretical practice, thus transforming the sciences into an instance above the historical process. The reorganisation of his system in the texts commencing with *Lenin and Philosophy* has resulted in the elimination of epistemological categories from Althusser's theory of philosophy, the sciences and their relation to the class struggle. However, the tension survives, displaced on to his theory of ideology, which presents a contradictory aspect as a theory of ideologies materialised in specific practices, the site and reflection of class struggles, hypostatised into a sociologistic theory of ideology in general.

The contradictory character of Althusser's work makes straightforward conclusions difficult. We have seen something of the relationship between Althusser's closet Stalinism and the tensions in his theoretical position. Because, in the last instance, his work is structured by the tension referred to in the previous paragraph, and because this tension has serious political consequences, Althusser's position as such must be rejected by Marxists.

Yet, at the same time we must accept that Althusser has made contributions of great importance to Marxist theory. His critique of Hegelian Marxism and his attempt to think, in the concepts of over-determination and structural causality, a materialist dialectic that is radically non-teleological and that captures the complexity of contradiction are achievements of lasting value. Moreover, he has provided us with elements of a theory of the sciences which is radically non-positivist and non-empiricist, which avoids the speculative ambitions of epistemology, and which enables us to think the sciences both in their specificity and in their relation to the class struggle. In the case of both his dialectical investigations and his theory of the sciences we should, however, recognise that Althusser's chief merit lies in having reformulated the problems that have to be solved in a useful way, rather than in providing any clear-cut solutions. The concept of problematic should have taught us, though, that this is not a minor achievement.

But unfortunately the matter cannot be left there. One of the principal gaps in Althusser's work, registered but not filled in his more recent writings, is his failure to discuss the unity of theory and practice. This is no mere theoretical omission. In this absence, this fracture, in Althusser's theory, we can read the political underplot of his work most clearly. The unity of theory and practice is the central problem of Marxist politics. And it is the central problem facing us, Marxists, today. The long boom is over, leaving in its wake crisis and the greatest threat to international capitalism since the era of the Russian Revolution. Imperialism faces a workers' movement that is on the offensive in all corners of the globe: Italy, Argentina, Southern Africa, Spain. In Portugal it is presented with the distinct possibility of a workers' dictatorship in the immediate future. If revolutionary politics and the mass struggles of the working class met and joined, they could detonate an explosion that would bring down capitalism. How to make them meet and join, how to build in the centres of working-class struggle across the globe revolutionary parties that can lead the international proletariat to state power, is the question that confronts Marxists from Bombay to Birmingham. To evade the issue of the unity of theory and practice today is to move away from Marxism.

The political reasons for Althusser's evasion of the issue should be evident. To pose the question of the revolutionary party today means breaking politically with Stalinism, since it means criticising, understanding and rejecting the reformism of the western Communist

103

Parties and the state capitalist bureaucracies of the eastern Communist Parties. This is something Althusser is not prepared to do.

The relation between this political stance and Althusser's theoretical position ought also to be clear from what has gone before. Althusser himself provides us with the tools for analysing this relation. He writes of the development of the young Marx's thought:

> It can be said that in this process, in which the *object* occupies the forestage, it is the political (class) position that occupies the determinant place, but the philosophical position that ensures the theoretical relationship between the political position and the object of reflection.[1]

In Althusser's case the relation between Marx and Hegel, i.e. the problem of the dialectic, is the object of his reflection. What concerns us here is the relation between his philosophical position, which has exercised us through most of this essay, and his political position, since according to him the latter is determinant in the last instance at the philosophical level.

This relation can be traced in his very theory. It is present in the contradiction between his critique of epistemology and his employment of epistemological categories. For we have seen that the tendency deriving from this contradiction is to separate off the sciences, to be specific, historical materialism, from the class struggle. It is thus that the unity of theory and practice is evaded, or solved only verbally, at the level of theory.

The effect of Althusser's practical, political evasion of the problem of revolutionary practice today upon his theoretical argument can be found even in his strengths. For it is precisely in the areas most separated from the problems of political practice – the structure of the dialectic, the nature of the sciences – that Althusser's positive achievements lie. Not that I wish to claim that the dialectic can be separated from the problems of political practice. Indeed it is at the point where the general question of the nature of the dialectic connects with practice that the most formidable problems are concentrated. This is, of course, the area of ideology. Everything links up somehow to ideology. The theory of overdetermination and the critique of empiricist epistemology hang together thanks to the treatment of fetishism as the necessary mode of existence of social relations. The obverse of history as a process without a subject is ideology as the instance that moulds individuals into subjects to fit the needs of this process. Science is defined in opposition to ideology. And ideology is vital in the process through which the problem of the unity of theory and practice is removed from our field of vision. For ideology is the way in which we relate to our conditions of existence, it is the way in which we live our relation to society. But the problem for revolutionary Marxists is to change the way in which people live their relation to society, to shift their stance from passive acquiescence to involvement in the struggle to overthrow capitalism and replace it with working-class self-government. How can a theory that treats people's relation to society as necessarily mystified accommodate this problem?

Finally, the theory of ideology effects a subtle shift in the treatment of the state. As I have already pointed out, Althusser only examines the problem of the state in relation to the theory of ideology. In discussing the problem of the superstructure he discusses the *Ideological* State Apparatuses, but not the state itself. While this approach may be valid from a limited, analytical point of view, and while the theory of the ISAs is in itself a useful one, we should be aware of the dangers here. Marxist politics is defined by its objective: the destruction of the bourgeois state apparatus and its replacement by the dictatorship of the proletariat in the form of a régime of workers' councils. Althusser's approach to the state carries with it the danger of replacing the struggle against the capitalist state by a struggle *in relation to* apparatuses which function to inculcate ideology, *at present* in the hands of the bourgeoisie, but which may be *taken over and used* to inculcate 'proletarian' ideology rather than bourgeois ideology. *This* attitude could well go hand-in-hand with an analysis of the state as a whole that places greater emphasis on its ideological than its repressive functions. Such an analysis would therefore redefine the role of proletarian revolution, shifting it from smashing of the capitalist state and replacing it with workers' power to changing the personnel in order to retool the machine and then pump out 'proletarian' ideology. The reformism of this approach and its consistency with the strategies of the Western

Communist Parties geared to coalition governments with capitalist parties ought to be clear.

Thus, on the questions that divide revolutionaries from reformists, the questions of the revolutionary party and the struggle against the capitalist state, Althusser is silent or misleading. It is on this score, ultimately, that Marxists must take up a critical stance towards his work.

Postscript

1974 was a good year for books by or about Althusser. Apart from Saul Karsz's useful if perhaps uncritical study of Althusser's philosophy, Althusser's 1967 lectures, *Philosophy and the Spontaneous Philosophy of the Scientists*, were published. Most important, however, was Althusser's *Eléments d'Autocritique (Elements of a Self Criticism)*. I only obtained and read this text after the final draft of my manuscript had been completed in January 1975. Since it is too important to be neglected, I have added this Postscript in order to discuss it.

Elements of a Self Criticism was written by Althusser in June 1972 as part of his reply to John Lewis, but was not published as part of that text so as to preserve its coherence. The *Self Criticism* concentrates upon a discussion of the philosophical position expounded in *For Marx* and *Reading Capital*, criticising it in the light of the theory of philosophy developed in *Lenin and Philosophy* and *Reply to John Lewis*. However, while it is something of an intellectual autobiography, as Althusser admits, he is concerned to emphasise its relation to the class struggle:

> Certainly, this self criticism whose 'logic' and *internal* arguments I am developing here as they have taken hold of our reflection, is not a purely internal phenomenon. It can only be understood as the effect of a *completely different, external, logic* that of the political events that I discussed in the *Reply to John Lewis*.[1]

Very little of this 'external' political logic can be found in the actual *Self Criticism*. Althusser concentrates upon isolating his theoretical errors and pursuing their consequences for philosophy and the science.

We should recall that Althusser has characterised the erroneous tendencies to be found in *For Marx* and *Reading Capital* as theoreticist and positivist: the assimilation of philosophy to science and its erection into a theory of theoretical practice with the effect of separating the sciences from the class struggle. We noted that what this meant was that the necessity and nature of the epistemological break became inexplicable. It is therefore appropriate that Althusser's self criticism should concentrate upon his treatment of the break in his earlier writings.

In criticising these writings, however, Althusser stressed that he does not reject the validity of the category of epistemological break nor does he in any way wish to qualify his stress upon the scientificity of Marxism. He stands by both the reality and the necessity of the rupture with bourgeois ideology and the construction of the first scientific concepts of historical materialism that Marx achieved in 1845. Indeed, he writes:

> It isn't an exaggeration to say that what is today at stake in the battle over these words ['science', etc. – AC] is *Leninism* as such. Not only the recognition of the existence and role of Marxist theory and science, but the concrete forms of the fusion of the Workers' Movement and Marxist theory, and the conception of materialism and of the dialectic.[2]

Althusser is here referring to his polemic against those who, like John Lewis, substituted humanism for class struggle as the basis of Marxism. But we know what to expect from the politics that Althusser would have us adopt: critical *gestures* (wrapped up in Maoist rhetoric) towards the reformism of the Communist Parties in the West, and the state capitalist tyrannies in the East.

But if Althusser still champions the epistemological break between Marxism and bourgeois ideology, what is his criticism of the version of it to be found in *For Marx* and *Reading Capital*? Essentially, that it remains a purely *epistemological* break, that is, an event that takes place purely *in theory*:

> But instead of giving this *historical* event [the break – AC] all its social, political, ideological and theoretical dimensions, I reduced it to the stature of a limited *theoretical* fact: the epistemological '*break*' observable in the works of Marx from 1845 onwards. Having done this, I

found myself caught up in a *rationalist* interpretation of the 'break' confronting *truth* and *error* in the shape of the speculative opposition of Science and Ideology in general, of which the antagonism between Marxism and bourgeois ideology became thus a particular case. Reduction + interpretation: the class struggle is practically absent from this speculative-rationalist stage.[3]

The rationalism of this treatment of the break lies in the fact that it reduces the break to an event at the level of the sciences alone. This reduction means that the break can only be explained in terms of factors internal to theory; the relation between the theoretical event and the totality of the social formation is broken. The sciences become a practice separate from the class struggle, enjoying a privileged existence in isolation from historical development.

How is this reduction effected? Through the reduction of the break to an opposition between Science and Ideology in general:

This is to bring into play there, confronting *science*, a Marxist notion that is very important, but very equivocal, and precisely in the form of its misleading equivoque in *The German Ideology*, where it plays, under the same undifferentiated name, two different roles, on the one hand, that of a philosophical category (illusion, error), and on the other hand that of a scientific concept (superstructural formation): the notion of *ideology*. And it matters little that *The German Ideology* authorises this confusion: since Marx abandoned it, and enabled us to avoid this trap. This was in fact to put in place this equivocal notion of ideology on *the rationalist stage* of the opposition between error and truth. And it was thus reducing ideology to error, and contrariwise baptising error ideology, giving to this rationalist theatre the usurped allures of Marxism.[4]

Despite Althusser's claim to have provided the only fundamental and coherent criticism of his position, we have seen that Rancière identified precisely the same error, the treatment of ideology as the illusion of science's truth. In general, we have seen that the *epistemological* treatment of ideology that remains constant throughout Althusser's writings is the link between the errors in his theoretical position and his Stalinist politics. The effect of this rationalist treatment of the break is to insulate the sciences from the rest of the social formation. But this cuts across Althusser's conception of science as the working over of pre-existing theory by a scientific problematic in order to produce new knowledges. This model requires that the conditions for the emergence of scientific problematics (Generalities II) can only come from outside scientific practice itself. Yet Althusser now admits that by cutting the sciences off from the social whole he made the construction of a scientific problematic an inexplicable mystery:

> I had thus certainly noted the existence of the 'break', but as I thought it under the Marxist disguise of error as ideology, and despite all the history and the dialectic that I tried to 'inject' into it, into the categories [truth and error – AC] that were, in the final analysis rationalist, I could not explain what had brought about this break, and if basically I was aware of it, I was incapable of thinking it and expressing it.[5]

The effect of this error was an attempt to theorise it, which resulted in the full flowering of Althusser's theoreticist deviation. This deviation was expressed in three theses. Firstly, there was the theory of the difference between Science and Ideology in general, a reversion to the problematic of guarantees that he had rejected. Secondly, there was the category of theoretical practice, which suppressed the distinction between the sciences and philosophy under the guise of an analysis of theory as production. Thirdly, there was the thesis of philosophy as the theory of theoretical practice, 'the culminating point of this theoreticist tendency'.[6]

Althusser goes on to discuss the accusations of abandoning Marxism for structuralism that were aimed at *Reading Capital* in particular, and which centred around the notion of structural causality, the notion of a cause that consists in the relation that its effects take up. Althusser argues that he had always rejected structuralism, which inasmuch as it is a homogeneous tendency consists in the reduction of reality to a combinatory of elements that possess no necessary relationship and the attempt to model reality in the abstract. He argues that the role of science is to render comprehensible concrete reality by means of a detour in theory, through the construction of abstract concepts in order to know the real, not to reduce it to the abstract. If he

110

cocquetted with structuralist terminology in *Reading Capital* he nevertheless never surrendered to structuralism.

Yet his discussion of *Reading Capital* in the *Self Criticism* does contain a significant retreat. He argues that structural causality remains of value, in a number of ways. One is scientific:

> To say that 'the cause is absent' signifies ... in Historical Materialism, that the 'contradiction in the last instance' is *never present in person* on the stage of history ('the hour of determination in the last instance never comes') and that one cannot get hold of it directly, as if it were a 'person present'. It is a 'cause', but in a dialectical sense, in determining *what* is, on the stage of the class struggle, 'the decisive link' to seize.[7]

Another is philosophical:

> The dialectic *makes the ruling cause an absent one*, for it effaces, eclipses and 'surpasses' *the* pre-Hegelian, mechanist category of cause, conceived as *the* billiard ball in person, that one can get hold of, the cause identified as *the* substance, *the* subject, etc. The dialectic makes mechanist 'causality' absent, in *presenting* the thesis of a completely different 'causality'.[8]

Thus structural causality becomes, on the one hand, a reformulation of the concept of overdetermination, and, on the other, the demarcation point between explanations of society that treat it as a concatenation of discrete events or the emanation of a subject and the explanation of society in terms of a complex and contradictory structure. The specification of how the structure of the whole operates upon the parts remains an uncompleted task. The summit of Althusser's account of the problematic of historical materialism in *Reading Capital* is demoted to a more modest role.

Althusser argues that his principal error in *Reading Capital* was theoreticist rather than structuralist. The effect of this error was a most symptomatic absence: that of the class struggle. Indeed, 'There is hardly any matter of the class struggle *for itself* in *For Marx* and *Reading Capital*.'[9]

How does this relate to what we saw above about Althusser's

progressive rejection of the notion of an epistemology, of a theory that provides guarantees of the scientificity of knowledges, and its replacement by a theory of philosophy as the class struggle in theory, providing the link between the sciences and the class struggle? Very closely. Althusser states the contrast in somewhat different terms to those I used, but the point he makes is the same. He defines epistemology as 'the theory of the conditions and forms of scientific practice and of its history in the different concrete sciences'. However, he distinguishes between two senses of epistemology. One is the speculative sense: 'The theory of Scientific Practice in its difference with other practices.' Here, of course, we have epistemology in the sense that I have used it in my essay, a philosophical ideology of the guarantee of scientificity to knowledges provided by the construction of a general criterion of scientificity. The other sense is the materialist: epistemology becomes the study of 'the material, social, political, ideological and philosophical conditions of the theoretical "modes of production" and "processes of production" of existing knowledges'.[10]

Thus a materialist epistemology becomes, in place of the metaphysical conditions prescribing the possible limits of any knowledge, the scientific analysis of the historical process through which the existing sciences have emerged. Althusser has sketched out what one aspect of such an analysis would look like in his text on the conditions of Marx's scientific discovery, which is now published in French for the first time with the *Self Criticism*.[11]

Althusser defines the conditions that, on this notion of a materialist epistemology, an analysis of the break would have to meet:

> The break doesn't explain itself, since it simply registers the simple fact of the symptoms and effects produced by a theoretical event, the historical emergence of a new science. But this event of theoretical history must still be explained by the conjunction of the material, technical, social, political and ideological conditions that brought it about. And, among these conditions, it is necessary, in certain cases, and incontestably in the case of Marx, to place in the front rank, the intervention of *theoretical class positions*, or what one can call the intervention of 'the philosophical instance'.[12]

Thus, a symptomatic reading becomes doubly symptomatic. It seeks to decode the presence of a theoretical problematic in the text, and to discover in that presence the symptoms of the historical conjuncture that caused the emergence of that problematic. In this conjuncture, the decisive role is played by philosophy, the class struggle in theory, as the theoretical form in which the confrontations between the different social classes are fought out, thus making possible, or hindering, the progress of the sciences.

The conclusion that Althusser draws from his *Self Criticism* is that while *For Marx* and *Reading Capital* contain the theoreticist deviation that he discusses, nevertheless their principal tendency, stressing as it does the scientificity of Marxism, remains correct. However, he admits that the effect of this theoreticism is to make them innocent of the class struggle. This is not a minor deviation. If Althusser now stresses that the class struggle is what Marxism is about, and if he attempts in his more recent writings to relate the class struggle to the emergence of historical materialism, the relation between Marxism and the working class remains displaced in his work.

This displacement has, as we have seen, shifted from the idealist theory of the sciences that he now rejects to the theory of ideology, which remains, despite the development of the theory of Ideological State Apparatuses, at heart an epistemological theory. In the *Self Criticism* Althusser recognises the contradiction between the epistemological conception of ideology as the other of science, and the materialist theory as the result and the site of class struggles. Indeed, he criticises the theory of ideology of *For Marx* and *Reading Capital* in these terms:

> I saw ideology as the universal element of historical existence: and I did not go any further. I thus left out of account the differences between the regions of ideology, and the antagonistic class tendencies that traverse, divide, regroup and confront them.[13]

Well and good. But Althusser never discussed the extent to which this contradiction between the materialist and the epistemological conceptions of ideology remains to trouble his later work. Despite what he says, his latest texts indicate that he continues to treat ideology as 'the

113

universal element of historical existence'. Under communism, the producers will continue to labour in ideology, and to need those armed with science to guide them.

Thus, if Althusser's *Self Criticism* provides us with a useful clarification of various points, and confirms the assessment of the development of his work contained in this essay, it does not involve development beyond the positions that I have criticised. Therefore, the overall judgement of his position remains the same: despite the important positive contributions Althusser has made, it must be rejected.[14]

References

Introduction

1. Althusser (1965) p.9.

2. See Birchall (1974) for an account of the crisis of post-war Stalinism.

Obviously, this crisis *within* Stalinism was a reflection of developments in the societies of the Russian bloc, including the end of the phase of 'primitive accumulation' in Russia and workers' uprisings against the state capitalist régimes, beginning with Berlin in 1953 and Hungary in 1956. See Harman (1974).

3. See Chapters 1 and 4 below.

4. Obviously much light could be obtained from an examination of Althusser's intellectual milieu, the Paris of the 1960s and 70s. Despite his protests, there are certain parallels between the preoccupations of Althusser and those of figures like the anthropologist Levi-Strauss, the psychoanalyst Lacan, or the epistemologist Foucault. They appear to share a common preoccupation with the unconscious structures presupposed by the activities of human subjects, with the complex and opaque forms taken up by human discourse, with alternatives to a humanism that treats the conscious human subject as sovereign. The cross-fertilisation of ideas (the influence, say, of Lacan on Althusser, or of Althusser on Foucault) and their common debt to Freud are other arguments for a common treatment.

However, such a treatment, if pursued in depth, would reveal major differences. It would moreover, force us to examine 'structuralism's' relation to its precursors, embracing the work of Freud, the phenomenological schools of Husserl and Heidegger, the linguistics of Jakobson and Saussure, and figures like Hegel and Nietzsche. It would lead us to follow their successors in the Parisian intellectual scene, figures like Derrida and Kristeva, as well as their existentialist predecessors and opponents like Sartre. The sheer *range* involved, a vast chunk of European intellectual history, helps to explain the limits I have imposed on an essay aimed primarily at discussing what Althusser means for Marxists.

115

5. 'Orthodox Marxism . . . does not imply the uncritical acceptance of the results of Marx's investigations. It is not the "belief" in this or that thesis, nor the exegesis of a "sacred" book. On the contrary, orthodoxy refers exclusively to *method*. It is the scientific conviction that dialectical materialism is the road to truth and that its methods can be developed, expanded and deepened only along the lines laid down by its founders.' Lukacs (1923) p.1.

6. See Chapter 3 below.

7. See especially Chapter 3 and the Conclusion below.

1. Marxism and Philosophy / pp.10–29

1. Marx (1859) p.22.

2. This is not strictly true: the exceptions are, of course, the 1857 Introduction to the *Grundrisse* and the 1859 Preface to the *Contribution to the Critique of Political Economy*. However, neither of these texts offer any definitive statement by Marx of his philosophical position, but, rather, hints, immensely rich in the case of the 1857 Introduction, sometimes dangerously crude and misleading in the case of the 1859 Preface.

3. This version of empiricism is discussed critically in relation to the history of the sciences in Lakatos (1970). There are, however, other varieties of empiricism. Empiricism as such can be defined as the philosophical position that founds knowledge on an underlying relation between the theory and the reality it seeks to analyse. Of this, more below.

4. See the essay, *The Marxism of Rosa Luxemburg*, in Lukacs (1923).

5. Engels (1925) p.62.

6. See Engels (1888).

7. See, for example, Engels (1925) p.196.

8. *ibid* p.266.

9. For a useful and enlightening discussion of Engels's philosophy see Stedman Jones (1973).

10. See Colletti (1968).

11. K. Kautsky, *Das Erfurter Programm*, quoted in Colletti (1968) pp.55–56.

12. R. Hilferding, Preface to *Finance Capital*, quoted in Colletti, (1968) p.74.

13. See Marx and Engels (1955), the letters on pp.415ff, and pp.419ff.

14. For further details, see Colletti (1968) and Korsch (1970).

15. Lenin (1929–30) p.180.

16. Two provisos before I continue. In the first place, I shall only examine the general philosophical positions the Hegelian Marxists shared, and it is important to emphasise the theoretical and political differences that existed between them, Althusser's common characterisation of them as 'theoretical leftists' is

116

inept: thus, Gramsci never took the ultra-left positions within the Comintern that both Lukacs and Korsch did at certain stages during their careers.

In the second place, nothing I say in criticism of these thinkers should be taken as a denial of the considerable theoretical and political merits of their work. This is especially so in Gramsci's case, where the analyses of the role of politics and ideology have not been surpassed, and is also true, although to a lesser degree, in the case of Lukacs and Korsch.

17. Gramsci (1971) p.333.

18. *ibid* p.365.

19. *ibid* p.341.

20. Lukacs (1923) p.39.

21. *ibid* pp.121–2.

22. *ibid* p.168.

23. Hegel (1821) pp.12–13.

24. Lukacs (1923) p.101.

25. *ibid* p.168.

26. *ibid* p.70.

27. *ibid* p.51.

28. Gramsci (1971) p.368.

29. *ibid* p.392.

30. *ibid* p.445.

31. Marx (1894) p.817.

32. Marx (1953) pp.101–2.

33. See Chapter 3 below.

34. Marx (1894) pp.312–13.

35. See Chapters 3 and 4 and the Conclusion, below. I would like to clear up immediately one potential source of misunderstanding. To assert that the practice of the proletariat in the productive process is necessarily mystified is not to assert that the practice of the proletariat *as such* is mystified. It is to assert the need for an alternative *revolutionary* practice which takes the proletariat beyond the productive process to state power. This is not to deny that the latter practice has its roots in the former, or that a dialectic takes place between the two practices: this is what building the revolutionary party is all about. But it is to deny that the practice of the proletariat in the capitalist labour-process can serve as the epistemological foundation of Marxism.

36. Lukacs (1923) p.229.

37. See Revai (1925). Any comprehensive critique of the early Lukacs would involve a discussion of his treatment of the physical sciences as one-sided and abstract forms of capitalist reification. This position and its roots in

the irrationalist and reactionary philosophies prevalent in France and Germany in the late nineteenth and early twentieth centuries are very well dealt with in Stedman Jones (1971) and Colletti (1969b). See, also, p.55 below.

38. Lukacs (1923) p.197.

39. See, for example, Marx (1847) p.173.

40. For Lukacs's ultra-leftism over, for example, participation in parliament, see Lukacs (1972). For Lenin and Trotsky's positions, see Lenin, *Collected Works*, Vols. 30 and 31, Trotsky (1924). In the last two chapters of Lukacs (1923) and in Lukacs (1924) we see a development beyond this idealist theory of the party and of class consciousness. Unfortunately, this break was not sustained, as the miserable 1969 postscript to the latter text testifies. From the late 1920s onwards Lukacs remained firmly on the right wing of the Communist movement, a position which allowed him to collaborate with Stalinism and, indeed, serve as its intellectual tool. The only exception was his participation in Imre Nagy's ill-fated government in 1956.

41. We shall return to the category of the subject below, pp.65ff.

42. See Lukacs (1972) pp.134–43 and Gramsci (1971) pp.419–72. In my discussion of the Hegelian Marxists of the 1910s and 1920s I have not considered Lenin's *Philosophical Notebooks*, which were, after all, his reading notes on *The Science of Logic*. However, Lenin's preoccupations differed sharply from those of the Hegelians. He was concerned with what Hegel's dialectic had to contribute to the materialist philosophy already elaborated in *Materialism and Empirio-Criticism* – knowledge as an infinite process of approximation to the real. The conflation of the problems of the unity of theory and practice and of the relation between the sciences and reality characteristic of the Hegelians is not encountered here. To substantiate this claim would require a digression that would be out of place in this essay. But see Lecourt (1973).

43. Not, however, rejected by Lukacs as late as 1961, when he wrote: 'Since we have to do with a popular work written for the masses, no one could find fault with Stalin for reducing the quite subtle and complex arguments of the classics on these themes to a few definitions in schematic and textbook form.' (*Nuovi Argumenti*, October 1961, quoted in Conquest (1968) p.109.)

2. The System / pp.30–71

1. See pp.66–69 for more on the teleological nature of Hegel's dialectic.

2. Thus in the *Grundrisse* we can detect the first emergence of the concept of labour power. See Marx (1953) p.267. The *Grundrisse* also contains the famous 1857 Introduction, which is vital for a clear idea of Marx's theory of the sciences, and an influential analysis of pre-capitalist social formations. See Tribe (1974) for a discussion of the *Grundrisse* that underlines its limitations in comparison with *Capital*.

3. See Lukacs's 1967 preface to a collection of his early writings including *History and Class Consciousness* (Lukacs (1923) pp.xxxvi–xxxvii). It is Gramsci rather than Lukacs who anticipated the thesis of the *Manuscripts* that a materialist dialectic must rest on the notion of the mediation of man's relation to nature by labour. Thus see Gramsci (1971) pp.351ff.

4. For a recent restatement of this position see Walton and Gamble (1972).

5. This failure does in fact often occur; Meszaros (1970) is a case in point.

6. Althusser and Balibar (1968) p.16. This passage refers to a famous part of *The Assayer*: 'Philosophy is written in this grand book, the universe, which stands continually open to our gaze. But this book cannot be understood unless one first learns to comprehend the language and read the letters in which it is composed. It is written in the language of mathematics, and its characters are triangles, circles and other geometric figures without which it is humanly impossible to understand a single word of it; without these one wanders about in a dark labyrinth.' Galileo (1623) pp.237–38. See Althusser and Balibar (1968) pp.34–40 for a discussion by Althusser of the empiricist theory of knowledge.

7. Althusser and Balibar (1968) p.43.

8. *ibid* pp.14–15.

9. *ibid* p.14.

10. Althusser (1965) pp.38–39.

11. See pp.73–77 below.

12. See, for example, Bachelard (1949) p.51. For a lucid account of Bachelard's philosophy, see Lecourt (1969).

13. Althusser (1965) p.67n.

14. Althusser and Balibar (1968) pp.25–26.

15. *ibid*.

16. *ibid* p.28.

17. Marx (1885) p.16.

18. Marx (1856) Part III p.254.

19. *ibid* p.191.

20. Althusser and Balibar (1968) p.52.

21. *ibid* p.17.

22. See, for example, Hegel (1812–16) Volume I, p.53.

23. Althusser (1965) p.93.

24. Althusser and Balibar (1968) p.94.

25. Althusser (1965) pp.101–2.

26. *ibid* p.197.

27. See Marx (1867), p.81 n.l.

28. Althusser (1965) pp.201–2.

29. Althusser and Balibar (1968) pp.99–100.

30. Althusser (1965) p.113.

31. *ibid* pp.204–5.

32. *ibid* p.206.

33. It is from his failure to grasp these positive aspects of Hegel's system in comparison with previous idealist philosophers, that there derives Colletti's inability to produce any account of Hegel's contribution to the development of Marxism and his obvious difficulties in the face of the existence of a materialist theory of contradiction in Marx's work. See Colletti (1969b) and (1974). For more on the dialectic see pp.66–69 below.

34. Marx (1953) pp. 99–100. See also Marx (1956) Part II, pp.87–88.

35. Lenin (1929–30) pp.359–60. The italics are mine in the case of the first pair of brackets. The employment of the distinction between the unity and the identity of opposites to differentiate the Marxist from the Hegelian dialectics can be found in Godelier (1966) and Karsz (1974).

36. Althusser (1965) p.213. I shall return to the notion of the whole as existing in its effects.

37. A useful selection of which has been published under the title *Between the Two Revolutions*.

38. Althusser and Balibar (1968) p.186.

39. See Marx (1867) pp.71–84.

40. See Marx (1894) pp.814ff and Marx (1956) Part III pp.453ff.

41. This point is well made in Geras (1971).

42. Marx (1894) p.880.

43. Marx (1956) Part III p.484.

44. For a brilliant account of the light the theory of fetishism throws on Marx's dialectic see Rancière (1965).

45. Althusser and Balibar (1968) pp.188–89. For Spinoza's concept of immanent causality see Spinoza (1677) Book I Propositions XIV–XVIII and the commentary in Woolfson (1934) Chapter IX.

46. Althusser (1965) pp.166–67.

47. In Althusser (1970a).

48. Korsch (1970) p.62.

49. There is another option which I have ignored: that of asserting that there is a qualitative difference between the natural and the social sciences. All the

120

adherents of this position, who include Lukacs, Weber and such luminaries of the Frankfurt School as Jürgen Habermas, are in this the heirs of the neo-Kantian subjectivism fashionable in Germany in the last century. There is no trace of such a claim in Marx or Lenin.

50. Althusser and Balibar (1968) p.42.

51. Marx (1953) p.101.

52. See Lakatos and Zahar (1974).

53. See Althusser (1965) pp182–93 for the details of his account of theoretical practice.

54. Althusser and Balibar (1968) p.56.

55. See pp.65–66 below.

56. Althusser and Balibar (1968) p.56.

57. *ibid* p.62.

58. *ibid* p.59.

59. Debray (1973) p. 187. I am grateful to Alan Montefiore, thanks to whom I learned of this passage's existence.

60. See, for example, Hegel (1812–16) Vol.I p.67.

61. Lenin (1929–30) p.134. See also *ibid* p.98.

62. Althusser (1965) p.231.

63. *ibid* pp.233–34.

64. *ibid* p.235.

65. See p.65 above.

66. Althusser (1965) p.231.

67. Althusser (1970a) p.153.

68. *ibid* p.155.

69. *ibid* p.158.

70. *ibid* pp.141–42.

71. *ibid* p.162.

72. *ibid* p.168.

73. Althusser (1973b) p.94.

74. Althusser (1970b) p.181.

75. Hegel (1812–16) Vol.I p.83.

76. Althusser (1970b) p.181.

77. *ibid* pp.182–83.

78. *ibid* p.183.

79. For example, the following passage: 'The principal agents of this mode of production itself, the capitalist and the wage-labourer, are as such merely embodiments, personifications of capital and of wage-labour; definite social characteristics stamped upon individuals by the process of social production;

121

the products of these definite social production relations.' Marx (1894) p.880.

80. Althusser (1973b) p.93.

3. Epistemological Blues / pp.72–88

1. See pp.58–60 above.

2. See, for example, Althusser and Balibar (1968) pp.133–35.

3. See p.60 above.

4. See pp.33–34 above.

5. Althusser and Balibar (1968) p.34.

6. *ibid* pp.65–66.

7. Althusser (1965) pp.38–39.

8. See p.62 above.

9. i.e. the works of 1845 – the *Theses on Feuerbach* and *The German Ideology* – and the works of 1845–58 respectively. See Althusser (1965) pp.33–38.

10. Althusser and Balibar (1968) p.74.

11. *ibid* p.63. Or, as Bachelard put it: 'In studying origins, philosophers believe they can find creations.' Bachelard (1949) p. 113.

12. Althusser (1965) p.169.

13. Glucksmann was, to my knowledge, the first to have pointed this out. Thus, see Glucksmann (1967) p.135.

14. See Althusser and Balibar (1968) p.135.

15. This is the burden of Geras's lucid critique: see Geras (1972). See Hirst (1971) for criticisms of the notion of a theory of theoretical practice on much the same lines as those in the text.

16. Althusser (1965) pp.14–15.

17. Althusser and Bachelard (1968) p.8.

18. Althusser (1968) p.50.

19. *ibid* p.53.

20. Lenin (1908) p.116.

21. *ibid* p.122. For a masterly discussion of the relation between philosophy and the sciences as seen at work in Lenin's case, see Lecourt (1973).

22. Althusser (1968) p.61.

23. Althusser (1973b) p.11.

24. Althusser (1968) pp.64–65.

25. See Popper (1963) Chapter 1. On Freud, see Althusser (1964).

26. Althusser (1973b) p.56.

27. For the ideological functioning of philosophy as the Science of Sciences, see Althusser and Balibar (1968) and the Introduction to Lecourt (1972).

122

28. An oblique confirmation of this interpretation can be found in Popper (1963) Chapter 2.

29. The relation between the rupture inaugurated by Galileo and Platonist philosophy is discussed in Burtt (1924) and Koyré (1939) and (1943). The first text by Koyré also contains a discussion of Descartes' contribution to classical physics.

30. See Koyré (1939) Part III.

31. Althusser (1973b) p.55.

32. Althusser (1973a) p.7.

33. Althusser (1971) pp.7–8.

34. Althusser (1969) p. 96.

35. Althusser (1973a) pp.8–9.

36. *ibid* pp.9–10. A useful selection of Marx's early writings can be found in Marx (1971). See also Marx's own account of his theoretical and political development in the Preface to Marx (1859), and the selection in Marx and Engels (1970).

37. Althusser (1973a) p.10.

38. For a useful discussion of the social conditions necessary for the emergence of historical materialism, see Therborn (1973).

39. See pp.36–37 above.

40. Althusser (1968) p.43.

41. *ibid* p.62. This account of Althusser's new theory of philosophy was written before I had got hold of Althusser (1974a). This contains the course of lectures he gave at the Ecole Normale Superieure in 1967 in which the position outlined in this chapter was first publicly stated. No new light on Althusser's work is thrown by them, although they do spell out in more detail than elsewhere the strictly philosophical implications of the position.

42. See the third section of Lecourt (1972), where he suggests that Foucault (1969) contains elements of such a theory.

4. The Politics of Ambiguity / pp.89–101

1. See Birchall (1974).

2. See Bettelheim (1973). A complete English translation of the book from which this extract is taken, Bettelheim (1970) was due to be published in 1975. Balibar's collaboration with Bettelheim was taken by the editors of *New Left Review* as an example of the extremes to which Althusser's philosophy can lead! See the Introduction to the English translation of Glucksmann (1967) in NLR 72.

3. See Cliff (1955) and Harman (1969).

4. Cliff and Birchall (1968) pp.67–68.

5. See Rancière (1970).

6. See pp.62–66 and Chapter 3 above.

7. Althusser (1965) p.232.

8. *ibid* p. 235.

9. Gramsci (1971) p.323.

10. See pp.48–'50 above.

11. Althusser and Balibar (1968) pp.216–24.

12. Marx (1867) pp.78–79. For a discussion of this question see Geras (1971).

13. See Balibar (1973a) and (1973b).

14. See the discussion in Karsz (1974).

15. Rancière (1970) p.4.

16. See pp.31–33 above.

17. Rancière (1970) pp.2–3.

Conclusion / pp.102–106

1. See p.86 above.

Postscript / pp.107–114

1. Althusser (1974b) p.8.

2. *ibid* p.33.

3. *ibid* pp.14–15.

4. *ibid* p42.

5. *ibid* pp.38–49.

6. *ibid* p.51.

7. *ibid* p.56n.

8. *ibid* p.57n.

9. *ibid* p.94.

10. *ibid* p.51n.

11. Althusser (1973a), published in Althusser (1974b) under the title *Sur l'évolution du jeune Marx*. See pp.85–87 above.

12. Althusser (1974b) p.98.

13. *ibid* p.82.

14. Althusser's 'self-criticism' in his (1973b) and (1974b) provoked a number of hostile reactions on the French left. Two important examples of this type of reaction are found in Rancière (1974) and Vincent (1974). However, these critiques, which I got hold of too late to comment on in the main text of this essay, are of rather varied value. Rancière's text, written by

124

one of the collaborators in the first edition of *Reading Capital*, is of immense significance as an analysis of the role of Althusser's evolution on the French left, and will provide a starting point for any further discussions of Althusser's politics; however, any theoretical alternative Rancière might have presented is marred by his own position, which reveals all the worst aspects of Maoism — voluntarism, spontaneism, empiricism. Vincent's collection of essays by members of the Ligue Communiste Revolutionnaire, a French Trotskyist group, is very disappointing. Beyond quite an effective analysis of Althusser's relation to Stalinism, the collection reveals very little of theoretical value and is a mixture of flaccid polemic, sloppy argumentation and dogmatic reassertion of the greyest of Trotskyist orthodoxies ('the Fourth International had theoretically posed and resolved the majority of questions raised allusively by Althusser in the theoretical and political domain'). With enemies like that Althusser has little need of friends.

Biographical Note[1]

Louis Althusser was born on 16 October 1918 at Birmendrëis, near Algiers. He went to school in Algiers and Marseilles, where he joined the Catholic Youth movement, Jeunesse Etudiante Chrétienne in 1937. In 1939 he was called up for military service. He was captured in June 1940 and spent the rest of the war in a German prisoner-of-war camp. After the war, he returned to his studies at the Ecole Normale Supérieure in Paris. His thesis, 'The Notion of Content in Hegel's Philosophy', was prepared under the supervision of the philosopher Gaston Bachelard. He took his degree in 1948, and has taught at the Ecole Normale Supérieure ever since. In 1948 he also joined the Communist Party, of which he remains a member.

1. This biography is based on that in Karsz (1974) p.335.

Bibliography

All books are cited by the date of their first publication in that form.

Althusser, L.
(1964) *Freud and Lacan* in Althusser (1971)
(1965) *For Marx*, London 1969
(1968) *Lenin and Philosophy* in Althusser (1971)
(1969) *Preface to 'Capital' Volume One* in Althusser (1971)
(1970a) *Ideology and Ideological State Apparatuses* in Althusser (1971)
(1970b) *Marx's Relation to Hegel* in Althusser (1972)
(1971) *Lenin and Philosophy and Other Essays*, London 1971
(1972) *Politics and History*, London 1972
(1973a) *The Conditions of Marx's Scientific Discovery* in *Theoretical Practice*, 7/8, January 1973
(1973b) *Response à John Lewis*, Paris 1973
(1974a) *Philosophie et Philosophie Spontanée des Savants*, Paris 1974
(1974b) *Eléments d'Autocritique*, Paris 1974

Althusser, L. and others (1965) *Lire le Capital*, Paris 1973, (first edition)
Althusser, L. and Balibar, E. (1968) *Reading Capital*, London 1970, (second edition)
Bachelard, G. (1949) *Le Rationalisme Appliqué*, Paris 1970
Balibar, E. (1973a) *Self Criticism* in *Theoretical Practice*, 7/8, January 1973
(1973b) *Sur le dialectique historique* in *Pensée*, No.170, August 1973
Bettelheim, C. (1970) *Calcul économique et formes de propriété*, Paris 1970
(1973) *State Property and Socialism* in *Economy and Society*, November 1973

127

Birchall, I. (1974) *Workers against the Monolith*, London 1974

Bukharin, N. (1921) *Historical Materialism*, Ann Arbor 1969

Burtt, E.A. (1924) *The Metaphysical Foundations of Modern Science*, London 1949

Cliff, T. (1955) *Russia*, London 1970

Cliff, T. and Birchall, I. (1968) *France: the struggle goes on*, London 1968

Colletti, L. (1968) *Bernstein and the Marxism of the Second International* in Colletti (1969a)

(1969a) *From Rousseau to Lenin*, London 1972

(1969b) *Marxism and Hegel*, London 1973

Conquest, R. (1968) *The Great Terror*, London 1971

Debray, R. (1973) *Prison Writings*, London 1973

Engels, F. (1878) *Anti-Dühring*, Moscow 1947

(1888) *Ludwig Feuerbach and the End of Classical German Philosophy* in Marx and Engels (1968)

(1925) *Dialectics of Nature*, Moscow 1954

Foucault, M. (1969) *The Archaeology of Knowledge*, London 1972

Galileo (1623) *The Assayer* in *Discoveries and Opinions of Galileo*, New York 1957

Geras, N. (1971) *Essence and Appearance: Aspects of Fetishism in Marx's 'Capital'* in *New Left Review* 65, January-February 1971

(1972) *Althusser's Marxism* in *New Left Review* 71, January–February 1972

Glucksmann, A. (1967) *A Ventriloquist Structuralism* in *New Left Review* 72, March–April 1972

Godelier, M. (1966) *Rationality and Irrationality in Economics*, London 1972

Gramsci, A. (1971) *Selections from the Prison Notebooks*, London 1971

Harman, C. (1969) *How the Revolution was Lost*, London 1969

(1974) *Bureaucracy and Revolution in Eastern Europe*, London 1974

Hegel, G.W.F. (1812–16) *The Science of Logic*, London 1929

(1821) *The Philosophy of Right*, New York 1971

Hirst, P. (1971) *Althusser and Philosophy* in *Theoretical Practice*, 2 April 1971

Hyppolite, J. (1955) *Studies on Marx and Hegel*, London 1969

128

Karsz, S. (1974) *Theorie et Politique: Louis Althusser*, Paris 1974

Korsch, K. (1970) *Marxism and Philosophy*, London 1970

Koyré, A. (1939) *Etudes Galiléenes*, Paris 1966

(1943) *Galileo and Plato* in *Journal of the History of Ideas*, 1943

Lakatos, I. (1970) *Falsification and the Methodology of Scientific Research Programmes* in: Lakatos and Musgrave (1970)

Lakatos, I. and Musgrave, A. eds (1970) *Criticism and the Growth of Knowledge*, London 1970

Lakatos, I. and Zahar, E. (1974) *Why did Copernicus' Programme supersede Ptolemy's?* Offprint

Lecourt, D. (1969) *L'Epistémologie Historique de Gaston Bachelard*, Paris 1972

(1972) *Pour une critique de l'Epistémologie*, Paris 1972

(1973) *Une Crise et Son Enjeu*, Paris 1973

Lenin, V.I. *Collected Works*, Moscow

(1908) *Materialism and Empirio-Criticism*, Moscow 1947

(1929–30) *Philosophical Notebooks*, Lenin *Collected Works*, Vol. 38

(1971) *Between the Two Revolutions*, Moscow 1971

Lukacs, G. (1923) *History and Class Consciousness*, London 1971

(1924) *Lenin*, London 1970

(1972) *Political Writings* 1919–29, London 1972

Macchiocchi, M.A. (1969) *Letters from inside the Italian Communist Party to Louis Althusser*, London 1973

Marx, K. (1847) *The Poverty of Philosophy*, New York 1963

(1859) *A Contribution to the Critique of Political Economy*, Moscow 1971

(1867) *Capital* Volume I, Moscow 1970

(1885) *Capital* Volume II, Moscow 1956

(1894) *Capital* Volume III, Moscow 1971

(1953) *Grundrisse*, London 1973

(1956) *Theories of Surplus Value*, Moscow 1963–72

(1971) *Early Works*, London 1971

Marx, K. and Engels, F. (1968) *Selected Works*, Moscow 1968

(1970) *The German Ideology* Part One, London 1970

Meszaros, I. (1970) *Marx's Theory of Alienation*, London 1970

Popper, K.R. (1963) *Conjectures and Refutations*, London 1969

Rancière, J. (1965) *Le conception de critique et de critique de l'économie politique des 'Manuscrits de 1844' au 'Capital'* in Althusser and others (1968)

(1970) *On the Theory of Ideology* in *Radical Philosophy* 7, Spring 1974

(1974) *La Leçon d'Althusser*, Paris 1974

Revai, J. (1925) *A Review of Georg Lukacs' 'History and Class Consciousness'* in *Theoretical Practice* 1, January 1971

Spinoza, B. (1677) *Ethics*, London 1959

Stedman Jones, G. (1971) *The Marxism of the Early Lukacs* in *New Left Review* 70, November–December 1971

(1973) *Engels and the End of Classical German Philosophy* in *New Left Review* 79, May–June 1973

Therborn, G. (1973) *The Working Class and the Birth of Marxism* in *New Left Review* 79, May–June 1973

Tribe, K. (1974) *Remarks on the Theoretical Significance of Marx's 'Grundrisse'* in *Economy and Society* 1974

Trotsky, L. (1909) *1905*, London 1973

(1924) *The First 5 Years of the Third International*, New York 1972

Vincent, J.-M. (ed) (1974) *Contre Althusser*, Paris 1974

Walton, P. and Gamble, A. (1972) *From Alienation to Surplus Value*, London 1972

Woolfson, H.A. (1934) *The Philosophy of Spinoza*, New York 1969

Index

Carl Boggs

Gramsci's Marxism

Carl Boggs introduces Gramsci as the first marxist theorist to grapple with the problems of revolutionary change in advanced capitalist society and as the first to identify the importance of the ideological-cultural struggle against bourgeois values. He links the themes of the prison notebooks to Gramsci's earlier work as political activist and leader of the Communist Party of Italy.

This is the first introduction in English to Antonio Gramsci's political philosophy.

Complete list of
Pluto books available from:
Pluto Press Ltd, Unit 10 Spencer Court,
7 Chalcot Road, London NW1 8LH

In the USA, from:
Urizen Books Inc, 66 West Broadway,
New York, NY 10007

Martin Shaw

Marxism and Social Science
the roots of social knowledge

Martin Shaw argues that the crisis of the social sciences is not simply one of intellectual direction. It grows from the social sciences' roots in the industrial, educational and ideological systems of capitalist society discussed in this book. The solutions are not just theoretical – theory must be related to practice, within academic institutions as well as in the wider class struggle.

A companion volume to *Marxism versus Sociology: a guide to reading*, also by Martin Shaw.

Complete list of
Pluto books available from:
Pluto Press Ltd, Unit 10 Spencer Court,
7 Chalcot Road, London NW1 8LH

In the USA, from:
Urizen Books Inc, 66 West Broadway,
New York, NY 10007